The Best of Rose Elliot
The Ultimate Vegetarian Collection

The Best of Rose Elliot
The Ultimate Vegetarian Collection

hamlyn

Notes

Vegan recipes are labelled **Ⓥ**

Both metric and imperial measurements are given for the recipes.
Use one set of measures only, not a mixture of both.

Ovens should be preheated to the specified temperature. If using a
fan-assisted oven, follow the manufacturer's instructions for adjusting
the temperature. This usually means reducing the temperature by 20°C
(65°F). Grills should also be preheated.

Free-range medium eggs should be used unless otherwise specified. The
Department of Health advises that eggs should not be consumed raw.
This book contains some dishes made with raw or lightly cooked eggs.
It is prudent for more vulnerable people, such as pregnant and nursing
mothers, invalids, the elderly, babies and young children, to avoid
uncooked or lightly cooked dishes made with eggs.

Buy cheese with the vegetarian symbol to ensure it is made with
vegetarian rennet and buy vegetarian Parmesan-style cheese instead of
traditional Parmesan, which is not vegetarian. Always check the labels of
preprepared ingredients to make sure they do not contain non-vegetarian
ingredients such as gelatine.

Fresh herbs should be used unless otherwise stated. If unavailable
use dried herbs as an alternative but halve the quantities stated.

Salt and pepper: use sea salt and freshly ground black pepper, unless
otherwise specified.

This book includes dishes made with nuts and nut derivatives. It
is advisable for those with known allergic reactions to nuts and nut
derivatives and those who may be potentially vulnerable to these allergies,
such as pregnant and nursing mothers, invalids, the elderly, babies and
children, to avoid dishes made with nuts and nut oils. It is also prudent
to check the labels of preprepared ingredients for the possible inclusion
of nut derivatives.

Contents

Introduction

Welcome to my new vegetarian collection. It's such a pleasure to see the recipes from *Vegetarian Supercook* and *Veggie Chic* brought together in one book, and I think you'll agree that it's a real feast. I loved writing those two books, and looking through this new collection brings back so many memories. It is always fun trying out new ideas and getting the reaction of others – my husband, my daughters, my grandchildren, whoever is around – and I can rely on them all for frank comments and often very helpful suggestions. One such time was when I was experimenting with the recipe for Wild Mushroom Tempura: one of my daughters came in with several friends, so what began as a quiet evening recipe-testing 'home alone' turned into a memorable kitchen party, and one of my happiest-ever tasting sessions, full of laughter and fun. You can see the results on page 29.

But first, let me give you an idea of what else is in store in this beautiful book. Divided into nine chapters, roughly arranged in meal order, it begins with starters and ends with desserts and cakes, with meals for every occasion in between.

The Starters chapter begins with one of my most popular recipes: Goats' Cheese & Cranberry Parcels. Everyone loves this because it's so pretty, and also – like the majority of the recipes in this book – so easy to make. And I must mention the Rosemary Sorbet,which is such a refreshing (and quite boozy) palate cleanser between courses.

In Classics with a Twist, you'll find variations on conventional dishes. Veggie versions of meat dishes, such as Lentil Shepherd's Pie with Smoky Cheese Mash; funky updates of vegetarian classics such as Thai-flavoured Mushroom Stroganoff with Golden Rice; and some very delectable lower carb versions of favourite recipes, such as No-rice Nori Sushi, Omelette Cannelloni with Spinach Filling and Tagliatelle of Cabbage with Cream Cheese, Herb & Garlic Sauce.

Although most of the recipes in this book are fairly quick to make (some very much so), the chapter to turn to, when you're short of time and want something fast and tasty, is Midweek Meals. These include speedy, rather snacky dishes that you could eat straight from the pan, such as Corn Fritters with Tomato Sauce or Rosti with Apple Sauce (so yummy!).

I was writing *Veggie Chic* when my youngest daughter got married, and for the reception the caterer used the recipes that I was creating for the book. I still can't make any of them without being transported back to the hottest day of that year and one of the happiest days of my life. It was many people's first experience of a fully vegetarian wedding and I was told we made one or two converts that day. The caterer later told me he was continuing to use the recipes, which had become part of his repertoire.

Vegetarians often miss out at parties and receptions, so having some recipes for vegetarian canapés is particularly useful. The Baby Yorkshire Puddings with Nut Roast & Horseradish are always a sensation, as are the Mini Carrot & Cardamom Tarte Tatins – and there are plenty of others: vegetarian (or vegan) guests need never be neglected if you have this book.

Of course, there are some show-stopping main courses and desserts too: both the Wild Mushroom Roulade and Moroccan-flavoured Aubergine Wellington spring to mind as examples of the former, while as a final flourish the Dreamy Raspberry & Rose Pavlova and Berry Skewers with White Chocolate Dip always evoke gasps of delight and appreciation.

The Lemon & Almond Drizzle Cake – so simple, so fast to make, so loved by everyone who tries it – seems to have become one of the 'signature dishes' of *Veggie Chic*, just as Whiskey Cream Banoffi has with *Vegetarian Supercook*. You've just got to try them! If you want to know some of my personal favourites, I love the Little Lemon Cheesecakes with Blueberries because they're so quick to make, look so pretty and can easily be made vegan, too; and I love the Chilli Kulfi, which also work really well when made with the pouring vegan soya cream.

Coming back down to earth, literally as well as figuratively, I love eating outside and you'll find me there at the first hint of sunshine, probably enjoying something from the Al Fresco chapter of this book. If you're looking for something a bit different for a veggie barbecue, try Dough Ball, Haloumi & Olive Skewers or Baby Potatoes & Mushrooms on Rosemary Skewers.

It's often the little touches that make a meal memorable and special. I often include a great accompaniment as part of a recipe, but side dishes also have a chapter to themselves. These complement and enhance the dishes and many of them can also stand alone as starters, snacks or light main meals. Who could resist Roast Potatoes in Sea Salt & Balsamic Vinegar? Or Parsnips in Sage Butter?

In fact, I'm really encouraging you to try everything that appeals to you. If there's one thing I'd like to give you, through this book, it's confidence in yourself and your ability to make beautiful, tasty food. This – confidence – is what I find so many people lack. The answer, as with so many things, is practice! The more you cook, the more confident you become, and the more confident you become, the more you want to cook… you get quicker at doing the processes, and bolder with the flavourings. Remember to taste as you go – please use clean teaspoons and don't 'double dip'! – and make sure to add enough seasoning; I find that many people err on the side of caution and tend to under season food.

But having said that, whatever the cookery writer might say, the important thing is to make the food taste good to you! I recommend you read a recipe right through before starting, and if you can, visualize yourself doing each process. And even if things take an unexpected turn, such as a roulade splitting as you roll it up, or a soufflé sinking a bit, who's going to grumble? Garnish it prettily and present it with a flourish!

I do hope you will enjoy using this book. It really does come with my love! You are in my mind as I create, taste and write the recipes, and I hope you will like making them as much as I do. Enjoy the process; choose recipes that really appeal to you and make you feel upbeat and happy; change some of the ingredients or flavourings to suit you – have fun. I wish you happiness, confidence and many wonderful veggie meals.

Rose Elliot

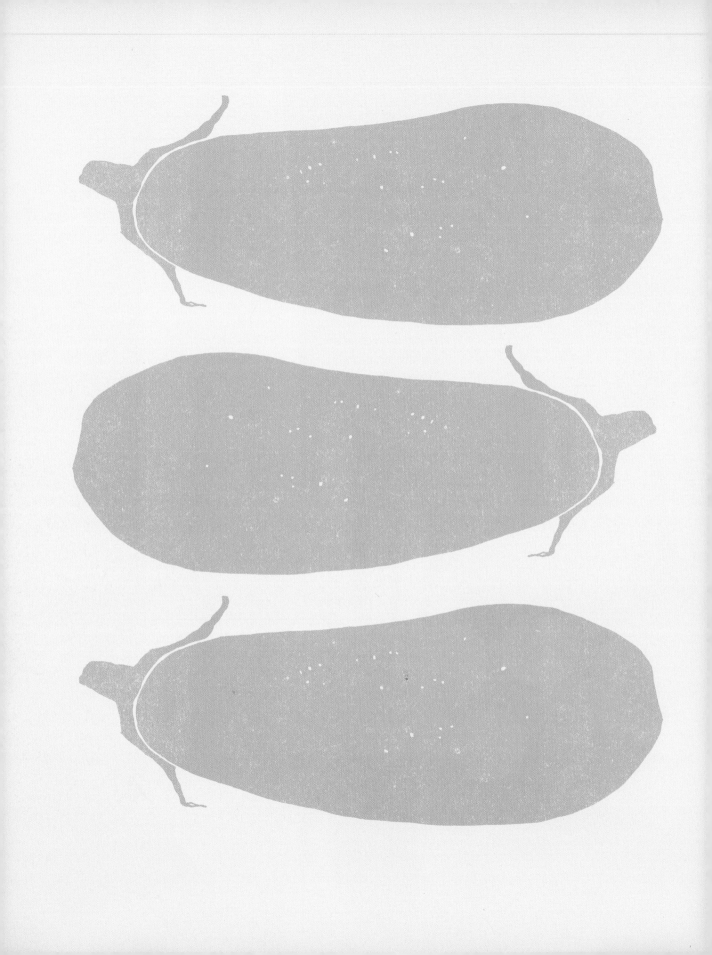

Starters

Goats' cheese & cranberry parcels

SERVES 4
PREPARATION 15 MINUTES
COOKING 15–20 MINUTES

4 sheets of filo pastry, 40 x 23 cm
(16 x 9 inches)
2 x 100 g (3½ oz) cylindrical
goats' cheeses
3–4 tablespoons olive oil, plus extra
for greasing
4 heaped teaspoons cranberry sauce
leafy salad and vinaigrette dressing
(see page 66), to serve

1 Cut each piece of filo into 4 quarters. Cut the cheeses in half widthways.

2 To make a parcel, put one of the pieces of filo on a work surface and brush with olive oil. Put another piece over it at right angles to make a cross and brush with olive oil again. Lay a third piece diagonally, as if you were making a star shape, brush with oil, then top with the final piece, diagonally, to complete the 'star', and brush with oil.

3 Place one of the pieces of cheese, cut-side up, in the centre of the pastry and put a heaped teaspoon of cranberry sauce on top of it. Fold up the sides of the filo and scrunch them at the top so they hold together. Brush all over with olive oil. Make 3 more parcels in the same way.

4 Place all the parcels on a lightly oiled baking sheet and bake in a preheated oven, 200°C (400°F), Gas Mark 6, for 15–20 minutes, or until crisp and lightly browned. Serve at once with a leafy salad dressed with vinaigrette – I think a chicory and watercress salad goes well as the bitterness contrasts with the sweet cranberry sauce. Alternatively, if you have the time to make them, some creamy mashed potatoes and fine green beans go well with the parcels.

Hot hazelnut-coated Vignotte
with redcurrant relish

SERVES 4
PREPARATION 10 MINUTES
COOKING 5 MINUTES

2 x 150 g (5 oz) Vignotte cheeses
100 g (3½ oz) skinned hazelnuts,
   chopped
1 egg, beaten
salad leaves and vinaigrette dressing
   (see page 66), to serve

FOR THE REDCURRANT RELISH

100 g (3½ oz) redcurrants
1 tablespoon caster sugar
squeeze of lemon juice

1 Remove any labels stuck on the cheeses, then cut them widthways into 4 rounds, retaining the rind. Spread the hazelnuts out on a plate.

2 Dip the rounds of cheese first in the beaten egg, then into the hazelnuts, making sure that all surfaces are thickly coated. Put the pieces of coated cheese on to a sheet of nonstick baking paper and chill until required.

3 To make the relish, put the redcurrants with the sugar and lemon juice into a saucepan. Bring to the boil, then remove from the heat and set aside.

4 Just before you want to serve the meal, transfer the cheese to a baking sheet and cook, rind-side down, under a preheated hot grill for about 5 minutes, or until the nuts are crisp and golden brown. Gently reheat the redcurrant relish.

5 While the cheese is cooking, line 4 plates with a few salad leaves and drizzle them with a little of the vinaigrette.

6 Serve the sizzling pieces of cheese on top of the leaves, with some of the redcurrant relish spooned on top and the rest in a small bowl.

Tomato & Parmesan tarts
with basil cream

SERVES 4

PREPARATION 15 MINUTES,
   PLUS STANDING FOR THE BASIL
   CREAM, IF POSSIBLE

COOKING 35 MINUTES

375 g (12 oz) frozen ready-rolled
   all-butter puff pastry (see page
   295)

40 g (1½ oz) Parmesan-style
   cheese, grated

450 g (14½ oz) cherry tomatoes,
   halved

2 teaspoons caster sugar

salt and pepper

FOR THE BASIL CREAM

bunch of basil, stems removed,
   leaves lightly chopped

6 tablespoons single cream or
   olive oil

1 To make the basil cream, mix the basil with the cream or olive oil, season with a little salt and pepper and leave to stand – this gets better and better as it stands, so can be made some hours in advance if convenient.

2 Spread the pastry out on a board and cut into circles to fit 4 x 10 cm (4 inch) shallow round loose-based flan tins.

3 Put the pastry into the flan tins and trim the edges as necessary. Prick the pastry all over with a fork. Bake in a preheated oven, 200°C (400°F), Gas Mark 6, for 15 minutes until golden brown – the pastry will puff up, so press it down gently with the back of a spoon. Remove the flan cases from the oven.

4 Sprinkle the Parmesan over the top of the flans – this keeps the pastry dry and crisp. Toss the tomatoes with the sugar and some salt and pepper and divide them between the flan cases – fill them generously as the tomatoes will shrink a bit as they cook.

5 Put the flans back into the oven and bake for 20 minutes. Remove the flans from their tins, place on warmed plates and swirl some of the basil cream over the top of each one. Serve at once.

Bloody Mary jellies

These jellies are best made not too far in advance and kept in a cool place rather than in the refrigerator. This recipe can be vegan if you use non-dairy horseradish sauce and soya cream from a healthfood shop.

SERVES 4

PREPARATION 15 MINUTES,
  PLUS SETTING

COOKING 2 MINUTES

400 ml (14 fl oz) tomato juice

1 teaspoon vegetarian gelatine
  (Vege-Gel, see page 296)

1½ tablespoons lemon juice

6 tablespoons vodka

2 teaspoons vegetarian Worcestershire
  sauce (see page 296)

½ teaspoon Tabasco

2 tablespoons each finely chopped
  red onion, celery and green
  pepper, plus a little more chopped
  red onion and celery, to garnish

1 tablespoon horseradish sauce

3 tablespoons single cream

salt and pepper

1 Put the tomato juice into a saucepan, gradually scatter the gelatine over the cold juice and stir until it has dissolved. Slowly bring to the boil, then remove from the heat immediately and stir in the lemon juice, vodka, Worcestershire sauce, Tabasco and some salt and pepper.

2 Divide the chopped vegetables between 4 small bowls or glasses. Pour the tomato jelly on top and leave to set for at least 30 minutes. Cool until required but don't refrigerate.

3 To serve, mix the horseradish sauce with the cream and swirl some over the top of each jelly. Scatter a little chopped red onion and celery over each one to garnish.

Rosemary sorbet ⓥ

Serve as a light starter or as a palate refresher between courses. Be warned – it's quite alcoholic.

SERVES 4
PREPARATION 15 MINUTES,
    PLUS COOLING AND FREEZING
COOKING 2 MINUTES

450 ml (¾ pint) water
150 g (5 oz) caster sugar
5 rosemary sprigs
250 ml (8 fl oz) white wine
4 tablespoons lemon juice
a few small sprigs and flowers of
    rosemary, to decorate (optional)

1 Put the water and sugar into a saucepan with 4 of the rosemary sprigs and bring to the boil. Remove from the heat, cover and leave to cool and infuse the flavour of the rosemary.

2 Remove the rosemary from the cooled syrup and stir in the wine and lemon juice. Chop the remaining sprig of rosemary and stir in.

3 Pour the mixture into a shallow container and freeze for about 2 hours, or until firm, scraping down the sides and whisking as it solidifies. Alternatively, freeze in an ice-cream maker until the mixture is soft and slushy, then transfer to a plastic container and freeze until required.

4 Remove the sorbet from the freezer about 15 minutes before you want to serve it, then scoop it into bowls and decorate with rosemary sprigs and flowers, if liked.

Aubergine & mozzarella scallops

Morsels of mozzarella wrapped in thin aubergine slices, crumbed and deep-fried, make a tasty starter, served with tomato sauce.

SERVES 4
PREPARATION 20 MINUTES
COOKING 30 MINUTES

1 fat aubergine, stem trimmed
olive oil, for brushing
75 g (3 oz) mozzarella cheese
1 egg, beaten
dried breadcrumbs, for coating
rapeseed or groundnut oil, for
   deep-frying
salt and pepper

FOR THE TOMATO SAUCE

1 tablespoon olive oil
1 onion, chopped
2 garlic cloves, finely chopped
400 g (13 oz) can chopped tomatoes

1 First make the tomato sauce. Heat the olive oil in a suacepan, add the onion, cover and cook for about 8 minutes, until almost tender. Add the garlic and cook for a further 2 minutes, then stir in the tomatoes and cook, uncovered, for about 20 minutes, or until very thick. Purée in a food processor or blender, then season and set aside.

2 Meanwhile, for the scallops, cut 20 rounds from the aubergine, making them as thin as you can – about 2.5 mm (⅛ inch) if possible. Brush them on both sides with olive oil and cook under a preheated hot grill for about 5 minutes, or until tender but not browned. Season them with salt and pepper.

3 Cut the mozzarella into 20 cubes, put one cube in the centre of an aubergine disc and fold the aubergine over like a mini Cornish pasty to make a 'scallop'. Dip in beaten egg, then dried breadcrumbs. Repeat with the remaining aubergine. Put the coated aubergine scallops on a piece of nonstick baking paper and chill until required.

4 Heat the rapeseed or groundnut oil in a wok to 180–190°C (350–375°F), or until a cube of bread browns in 30 seconds. Add the aubergine scallops and deep-fry until crisp and golden all over, turning them as necessary. Drain on kitchen paper.

5 Serve 5 on each plate, with the tomato sauce drizzled around the edge.

Spinach custards with avocado

SERVES 4
PREPARATION 20 MINUTES
COOKING 35–40 MINUTES

butter, for greasing
225 g (7½ oz) spinach
300 ml (½ pint) double cream
2 eggs
grated nutmeg
1 large ripe avocado
salt and pepper

FOR THE LEMON VINAIGRETTE

3 tablespoons lemon juice
9 tablespoons olive oil

1 Grease 4 x 125–150 ml (4–5 fl oz) ramekins, cups, individual pudding basins or other suitable moulds with butter and line the bases with circles of nonstick baking paper.

2 Wash the spinach, then place in a saucepan with just the water clinging to the leaves and cook for about 6 minutes, or until very tender. Drain well in a sieve, squeezing out as much water as possible, then chop.

3 Put the spinach into a food processor with the cream and eggs and whiz to a purée, then season with grated nutmeg, salt and pepper.

4 Pour the mixture into the prepared moulds, then stand them in a roasting tin and pour in boiling water around them to come halfway up the sides of the moulds. Bake in a preheated oven, 180°C (350°F), Gas Mark 4, for 30 minutes, or until firm on top and a skewer inserted into the centre comes out clean. Remove from the oven and leave to cool.

5 To make the vinaigrette, whisk the lemon juice with the olive oil and some salt and pepper.

6 Slip a knife around the edges of the moulds to loosen, then turn them out on to individual plates. Peel and slice the avocado and arrange some slices on each plate. Season with salt and pepper, then spoon the lemon vinaigrette over the avocado and the custards and serve warm or cold.

Vietnamese spring rolls ⓥ

These unusual spring rolls are made from rice pancakes and are served uncooked, with a spicy dipping sauce. They taste very fresh and delicious; serve as a starter or snack, or with Sesame-roasted tofu (see page 114) and rice.

SERVES 4

PREPARATION 30 MINUTES

50 g (2 oz) thin rice noodles
(one bundle from a packet)
150 g (5 oz) bean sprouts
1 red pepper, cored, deseeded
and finely sliced
2 teaspoons chopped mint
2 teaspoons chopped coriander
3 spring onions, finely chopped
3 tablespoons teriyaki sauce
8 rice flour pancakes

FOR THE PEANUT DIP

2 tablespoons crunchy peanut butter
2 teaspoons brown sugar
1 cm (½ inch) piece of fresh root
ginger, grated
1 garlic clove, crushed
¼ teaspoon dried red chilli flakes
6–8 tablespoons soy sauce

1 Put the noodles into a bowl, cover with boiling water and leave to soak for 5 minutes, until tender, then drain well and place in a bowl.

2 Add the bean sprouts, red pepper, mint, coriander, spring onions and teriyaki sauce and mix well, making sure the ingredients are well distributed.

3 Spread a clean damp tea towel over the work surface. Put the rice pancakes into a bowl, cover with hot water and leave to soak for about 20 seconds, or until they become flexible. Remove them from the water and spread them out on the tea towel.

4 Take about 2 tablespoons of the bean sprout mixture and place on one of the pancakes towards the edge nearest you. Fold in the 2 sides, then the bottom edge so that it covers the filling. Roll this over again, holding in the filling firmly, and keep rolling until you have a firmly packed spring roll. Put this on a plate, seam-side down. Continue in this way until all the pancakes have been used. Cover the finished rolls with the clean damp tea towel until required.

5 To make the dip, mix together the peanut butter, sugar, ginger, garlic and chilli, then gradually mix in the soy sauce. Put into 4 small bowls and serve with the spring rolls.

Polenta chip stack with dipping sauces

You can make these chips using ready-made polenta, which makes them very quick and easy, or you can make the polenta from scratch.

SERVES 4

PREPARATION 15 MINUTES–1 HOUR,
   DEPENDING ON THE TYPE OF
   POLENTA

COOKING 30 MINUTES–1¼ HOURS,
   DEPENDING ON THE POLENTA

500 g (1 lb) pack ready-made
   polenta or 175 g (6 oz) instant
   or traditional polenta
1 litre (1¾ pints) water
1 teaspoon salt
rapeseed or groundnut oil, for
   deep- or shallow-frying

FOR THE DIPPING SAUCES

4 heaped tablespoons mayonnaise
1 tablespoon sun-dried tomato paste
225 g (7½ oz) jar chunky salsa
1 large ripe avocado
3 tablespoons chopped coriander
juice of 1 lime
pinch of chilli powder
salt and pepper

1 If using ready-made polenta, blot with kitchen paper, then cut the polenta into chunky chips – a 500 g (1 lb) block will make 24.

2 Or, if using instant polenta, make as directed on the packet. For traditional polenta, heat the water and salt in a large saucepan. When the water comes to the boil, sprinkle the polenta over the surface, stirring all the time to prevent lumps. If you do get some lumps, whiz them away with a stick blender or whisk. Leave the mixture to simmer for 45 minutes, or until very thick, stirring from time to time.

3 Line an 18 x 28 cm (7 x 11 inch) Swiss roll tin with nonstick baking paper. Pour the polenta into the tin, spreading it to the edges and into the corners. Leave to cool and firm up.

4 Meanwhile, make the dipping sauces. Mix the mayonnaise with the tomato paste and put into a small bowl. Put the salsa into another bowl. Remove the stone and skin from the avocado and mash the flesh with the coriander, lime juice, chilli powder and some salt and pepper to make a creamy, slightly chunky consistency. Put into a bowl.

5 Cut the firm polenta into chips about 15 cm (6 inches) long and 1 cm (½ inch) wide. Pour enough oil into a frying pan to cover the polenta chips and heat to 180–190°C (350–375°F), or until a cube of bread browns in 30 seconds, then shallow- or deep-fry them. It's easy to keep them separate if you shallow-fry them, but make sure they're submerged in oil and cook them until they are really crisp and golden on one side, then turn them over and cook the other side thoroughly. Drain on kitchen paper. If you get them very crisp, the first batch will stay crisp while you fry the rest – keep them warm on kitchen paper in a cool oven.

6 Pile the polenta chips into a stack on a serving dish – or on individual plates – and serve with the 3 dipping sauces.

Adzuki, rice & ginger balls with teriyaki dip ⓥ

MAKES 18
PREPARATION 20 MINUTES
COOKING 1 HOUR 5 MINUTES

50 g (2 oz) adzuki beans
125 g (4 oz) brown rice
2 teaspoons grated fresh root ginger
300 ml (½ pint) water
2 teaspoons lemon juice
flesh from 2–3 umeboshi plums or
    1–2 teaspoons umeboshi paste (see
    page 296)
2–3 tablespoons sesame seeds
salt and pepper

FOR THE DIP

3 tablespoons shoyu or tamari
3 tablespoons mirin

1 Put the beans into a saucepan, cover with water and bring to the boil, then reduce the heat, half cover the pan and simmer for 45 minutes, or until tender. Drain.

2 Meanwhile, put the rice and ginger into a saucepan with the measured water. Bring to the boil, then reduce the heat, cover and leave to cook over a very gentle heat for 30–40 minutes, or until the rice is tender and all the water has been absorbed.

3 Put the rice into a food processor with the adzuki beans, lemon juice, umeboshi and some salt and pepper and whiz to a thick mixture that holds together.

4 Put the sesame seeds on to a large plate, then break off large marble-sized pieces of the rice mixture and roll them in the seeds to form 18 balls. Place the rice balls on a baking sheet and bake in a preheated oven, 180°C (350°F), Gas Mark 4, for 20 minutes, or until crisp on the outside.

5 To make the dip, mix the shoyu or tamari with the mirin in a small bowl and serve with the rice balls.

Wild mushroom tempura with garlic mayonnaise ⓥ

Provided you buy a vegan mayonnaise, this makes a luxurious vegan main course – the unusual tempura batter is light and very crisp. A bag of mixed wild mushrooms from a supermarket is perfect for this recipe.

SERVES 4
PREPARATION 15 MINUTES
COOKING 30 MINUTES

500 g (1 lb) mixed wild mushrooms,
    torn into bite-sized pieces
rapeseed or groundnut oil,
    for deep-frying
garlic mayonnaise or aioli, to serve

FOR THE TEMPURA BATTER

100 g (3½ oz) plain white flour
200 g (7 oz) cornflour
3 teaspoons baking powder
200 ml (7 fl oz) sparkling water
salt

1 Just before you want to serve the mushrooms, heat sufficient rapeseed or groundnut oil in a deep-fat fryer to 180–190°C (350–375°F), or until a cube of bread browns in 30 seconds.

2 While the oil is heating, make the batter. Put the flour, cornflour and baking powder into a bowl with some salt. Pour in the water and stir the mixture quickly with a fork or chopstick to make a batter.

3 Dip pieces of mushroom into the batter, then put them into the hot oil and deep-fry for 1–2 minutes, until they are golden brown and very crisp. Drain on kitchen paper. You will need to cook in batches, but the first ones will stay crisp while you fry the rest.

4 Pile the tempura on a plate and serve immediately with the garlic mayonnaise or aioli.

Red pepper hummus with smoked paprika

Using sweet peppers from a jar makes this recipe very quick and easy. Smoked paprika gives an intriguing, unusual flavour, but if you can't find it use mild paprika instead.

SERVES 4
PREPARATION 15 MINUTES

2 garlic cloves
410 g (13½ oz) can chickpeas, drained
½ x 325 g (11 oz) jar whole sweet red peppers, drained
1 teaspoon honey
Tabasco, to taste
¼–½ teaspoon smoked paprika
coarsely ground black pepper and warm or griddled pitta bread, to serve

1 Put the garlic cloves into a food processor and whiz until chopped, then add the chickpeas, red peppers and honey and whiz again. Stir in the Tabasco and smoked paprika to taste.

2 Turn the mixture on to a flat plate and smooth the surface. Grind some black pepper coarsely over the top and serve with strips of warm or griddled pitta bread.

Fruity guacamole •ᵥ•

An authentic Mexican twist on an old favourite – a wonderful taste explosion of hot and salty, sweet and sour. This guacamole makes a wonderful starter, but you must prepare it just before serving for the best colour.

SERVES 4
PREPARATION 25 MINUTES

1 large garlic clove
1 green chilli, deseeded
1 bunch of coriander, stalks removed
juice and pared or grated rind
    of 1 lime
2 ripe avocados, peeled, stoned
    and roughly chopped
1 pomegranate
1 ripe peach, peeled, stoned
    and chopped
salt
2 little gem lettuces, leaves separated
    and hearts quartered, to serve

1 Put the garlic and chilli into a food processor with most of the coriander, saving a few coriander leaves for garnishing. Whiz until finely chopped. Add the lime rind and juice (perhaps holding back a few strands of rind to garnish), the avocados and a little salt and whiz to a green cream. Transfer to a mixing bowl.

2 Cut the pomegranate in half and bend back the skin – as if you were turning it inside out – to make the seeds pop out. Gently fold most of the seeds and the chopped peach into the avocado mixture.

3 Arrange the lettuce leaves and hearts around the edge of a serving dish. Heap the guacamole on top, then lightly stud it with the remaining peach and pomegranate and scatter over the reserved coriander leaves and lime rind. Serve as soon as possible.

Refried beans

It's all the extras that make this very simple dish special. I like to serve them in little bowls so everyone can help themselves to what they want.

SERVES 4
PREPARATION 15 MINUTES
COOKING 15 MINUTES

2 tablespoons olive oil
1 large onion, finely chopped
2 garlic cloves, chopped
2 x 410 g (13½ oz) cans pinto beans,
   drained
½–1 teaspoon chilli powder
salt and pepper

TO SERVE

lettuce leaves
sliced tomatoes
1 large avocado, peeled, stoned
   and sliced
soured cream
paprika
chopped coriander
tortilla chips
grated Cheddar cheese (optional)

1 Heat the olive oil in a large, heavy-based saucepan, add the onion, cover and cook gently for 10 minutes, stirring from time to time. Stir in the garlic and cook for a minute or two longer.

2 Add the pinto beans to the pan, along with the chilli powder, salt and pepper to taste. Mash the beans roughly with a potato masher or wooden spoon so that they cling together, but keep plenty of texture. Stir well so that they don't stick to the pan. The beans are ready when they're piping hot.

3 Arrange some lettuce leaves on a large serving plate and spoon the beans into the centre. Arrange tomato and avocado slices around the edge, swirl soured cream, paprika and coriander on top and serve with tortilla chips and grated Cheddar, if liked.

Stilton pâté with roasted baby beetroots, dill & chicory salad

SERVES 4
PREPARATION 15 MINUTES
COOKING 1–1½ HOURS

450 g (14½ oz) baby beetroots,
    preferably no bigger than plums
olive oil, for rubbing
dill sprigs, to garnish
coarsely ground black pepper and
    rustic bread, to serve

FOR THE STILTON PÂTÉ

200 g (7 oz) low-fat soft
    cream cheese
1 teaspoon Dijon mustard
200 g (7 oz) Stilton cheese,
    roughly crumbled
1 tablespoon vegetarian port
    or sweet sherry
pepper

FOR THE SALAD

2–3 chicory
1 bunch of watercress
50 g (2 oz) walnuts

1 If the beetroots still have leaves attached, cut these off about 5 cm (2 inches) from the beetroot. Scrub the beetroots gently, being careful not to pierce the skin, and leave the long 'tail' on, if still attached. Rub the beetroots with a little olive oil, wrap them lightly in a piece of foil and bake in a preheated oven, 200°C (400°F), Gas Mark 6, for 1–1½ hours, or until tender right through when pierced with a knife. You could uncover them for the last 30 minutes or so, but you don't want them to get too crisp. I like to eat them skins and all, but most people rub off the skins before eating.

2 While the beetroot is cooking, make the pâté. Put the cream cheese, mustard, Stilton and port or sherry into a food processor and whiz to a cream. Season with a little pepper.

3 Mix the ingredients for the salad together.

4 To serve, put a spoonful of the Stilton pâté on each plate with some of the beetroot – baby ones can be left whole, larger ones cut as necessary – and one or two feathery leaves of dill. Grind some black pepper coarsely over the top and serve with the salad and rustic bread.

Nut & miso pâté with cranberry relish & dill ⓥ

This wonderful and unusual pâté was inspired by a recipe that appeared in the *Vegetarian Times*. Serve with strips of warm pitta bread.

SERVES 4
PREPARATION 20 MINUTES,
  PLUS SOAKING
COOKING 15 MINUTES

75 g (3 oz) cashew nuts
125 g (4 oz) firm tofu, drained
1 garlic clove, crushed
4 teaspoons red miso
1 tablespoon nutritional yeast
  (see page 295) or a little yeast
  extract, to taste
1 teaspoon shoyu or tamari
4 teaspoons lemon juice
white pepper
3 tablespoons chopped dill
4 dill sprigs, to garnish

FOR THE CRANBERRY RELISH

50 g (2 oz) dried cranberries
150 ml (¼ pint) full-bodied red wine
1 teaspoon olive oil
¼ teaspoon white mustard seeds
1 tablespoon finely chopped onion
1 garlic clove, finely chopped
1 teaspoon grated fresh root ginger
pinch of chilli powder
1 tablespoon caster sugar
1 tablespoon red wine vinegar
salt

1 First make the cranberry relish. Put the cranberries into a bowl, cover with the wine and set aside. Heat the olive oil in a small saucepan, add the mustard seeds, stir for a few seconds until they start to 'pop', then add the onion, garlic, ginger and chilli powder. Cook over a gentle heat for about 5 minutes, or until the onion is tender.

2 Add the cranberries and their liquid to the pan, along with the sugar, red wine vinegar and some salt. Bring to the boil, then reduce the heat and simmer, uncovered, for a few minutes, until the liquid has reduced and is syrupy and the cranberries are tender. Cool. (This will keep, covered, in the refrigerator for up to 2 weeks.)

3 For the pâté, put the cashews into a bowl, cover with cold water and leave to soak for 4–8 hours. Drain. Put into a food processor with the tofu, garlic, miso, yeast, shoyu or tamari, lemon juice and a good pinch of white pepper and whiz to a very creamy pâté. Scrape into a bowl, cover and set aside until required.

4 To serve, stir the chopped dill and 4 tablespoons of the cranberry relish into the pâté. Arrange a spoonful in the centre of each of 4 plates and garnish each with a dill sprig. Serve at once – the pâté loses its bright, fresh colour if left to stand.

Lentil & olive pâté with grilled fennel ⓥ

SERVES 4
PREPARATION 10 MINUTES
COOKING 10 MINUTES

4 fennel bulbs
2 tablespoons olive oil
lemon wedges, to serve

FOR THE PÂTÉ

2 garlic cloves
410 g (13½ oz) can green lentils,
   drained
150 g (5 oz) black olives, such as
   Kalamata, pitted

1 Trim the tops off the fennel, then, using a sharp knife or a potato peeler, shave off a thin layer of the outer bracts, to remove any tough threads. Cut the bulbs in half, then into quarters or sixths, depending on the size of the fennel. Brush the pieces on both sides with olive oil, place on a grill pan and cook under a preheated very hot grill for about 10 minutes, or until tender and browned, turning them as necessary.

2 Meanwhile, make the pâté. Put the garlic cloves into a food processor and whiz to chop, then add the lentils and black olives and whiz again to a thick, fairly chunky consistency.

3 Heap the pâté up on a plate, arrange the grilled fennel and lemon wedges around the edge and serve.

Soups & salads

Red lentil & roasted pepper soup

SERVES 6
PREPARATION 20 MINUTES
COOKING 40 MINUTES

2 red onions, cut into 2.5 cm
    (1 inch) pieces
2 teaspoons olive oil
2 red peppers, halved, cored
    and deseeded
4 garlic cloves, unpeeled
small handful of thyme
125 g (4 oz) split red lentils
600 ml (1 pint) water
2 bay leaves
salt and pepper
chopped basil, to garnish
a few shavings of Parmesan-style
cheese, to serve

1 Toss the onions in the olive oil and put them on a baking sheet, along with the peppers, which don't need oiling. Roast in a preheated oven, 180°C (350°F), Gas Mark 4, for 30 minutes, or until the vegetables are nearly tender, then add the garlic and thyme to the baking sheet and cook for a further 10 minutes, until all the vegetables are tender. Leave to cool.

2 Meanwhile, put the red lentils into a saucepan with the water and bay leaves. Bring to the boil, then reduce the heat and simmer for 15 minutes, or until the lentils are soft and pale coloured. Remove and discard the bay leaves.

3 Rub off as much of the skin from the peppers as you can – get rid of any very dark bits, but don't worry about being too particular. Pop the garlic out of its skin with your fingers. Put the peppers and garlic into a food processor with the onion (discard the thyme). Add the lentils together with their cooking liquid and whiz to a smooth, creamy consistency, thinning it with a little water, if necessary.

4 Return the mixture to the pan and reheat gently. Season to taste with salt and pepper, then ladle into warmed bowls and top each with basil and thin shavings of Parmesan.

Hot & sour mushroom soup ⓥ

This glamorous soup has a long list of ingredients but is incredibly quick to make! Use a medium-sized, long chilli for this – not the tiny, very hot bird's-eye type. Make sure the curry paste is vegetarian – read the label.

SERVES 4
PREPARATION 10 MINUTES,
   PLUS STANDING
COOKING 15–20 MINUTES

1 teaspoon vegetarian Thai
   red curry paste
125 g (4 oz) shiitake mushrooms,
   thinly sliced
1 small cluster of enoki mushrooms,
   base trimmed off
1 red chilli, deseeded and cut
   into rings
20 g (¾ oz) coriander, chopped
juice of 1 lime
2–3 tablespoons shoyu or tamari
salt

FOR THE THAI-FLAVOURED STOCK

2–3 lemon grass stalks, crushed
   with a rolling pin
6 kaffir lime leaves, plus 6 more to
   garnish (optional)
stems from a small bunch of
   coriander
2 thumb-sized pieces of fresh root
   ginger, peeled and sliced
1 litre (1¾ pints) water

1 To make the stock, put the lemon grass, lime leaves, coriander stems and ginger into a saucepan with the water. Bring to the boil, then reduce the heat and simmer for 10 minutes. Remove from the heat, cover the pan and leave to stand for 30 minutes or longer for the flavours to infuse, then drain the liquid into another pan and discard the flavourings.

2 Add the curry paste, mushrooms and red chilli to the stock, then reheat and simmer for 3–4 minutes, to cook the mushrooms and chilli.

3 Stir in the chopped coriander, lime juice, shoyu or tamari and some salt, then heat gently. Ladle into warmed bowls and garnish with a lime leaf, if liked.

Carrot & caraway soup ⓥ

Caraway, from the same plant family as carrots, gives this soup its subtle, unusual flavour and deserves to be more widely used. It also adds a lovely flavour to cooked, buttered carrots or beetroot.

SERVES 4
PREPARATION 15 MINUTES
COOKING 40 MINUTES

1 tablespoon olive oil
1 onion, chopped
1 baking potato, peeled and cut into
   1 cm (½ inch) cubes
500 g (1 lb) scraped carrots, sliced
2–3 strips of lemon rind
1 teaspoon caraway seeds
1.2 litres (2 pints) water or
   light vegetable stock
salt and pepper
fromage frais, natural yogurt or
   reduced-fat crème fraîche
   (optional) and coarsely ground black
   pepper, to serve
chopped flat leaf parsley, to garnish

1 Heat the olive oil in a large saucepan, add the onion, cover and cook gently for 5 minutes, stirring from time to time – don't let it brown.

2 Add the potato, cover and cook for a further 5 minutes, then add the carrots, lemon rind and caraway seeds. Stir well, then add the water or stock. Bring to the boil, then reduce the heat, cover and leave to cook gently for about 30 minutes, or until the carrots are very tender.

3 Purée the soup in a food processor or blender, then return the mixture to the pan. Season with plenty of salt and a little pepper and reheat gently.

4 Ladle the soup into warmed bowls and swirl a teaspoon of fromage frais, yogurt or crème fraîche on top of each, if liked. Grind some black pepper coarsely over the top, scatter with a little flat leaf parsley and serve.

Chunky bean & vegetable soup ⓥ

There are numerous versions of this Mediterranean soup, which is easy to make and deliciously wholesome. Feel free to try using different vegetables or perhaps adding some small pasta shapes.

SERVES 4
PREPARATION 15 MINUTES
COOKING 45 MINUTES

1 tablespoon olive oil
2 onions, chopped
250 g (8 oz) carrots, cut into 1 cm
   (½ inch) chunks
250 g (8 oz) parsnips, cut into 1 cm
   (½ inch) chunks
250 g (8 oz) leeks, sliced
250 g (8 oz) cabbage, sliced
a few thyme sprigs
2 bay leaves
410 g (13½ oz) can cannellini beans,
   drained
1.2 litres (2 pints) vegetable stock
salt and pepper
chopped parsley, to garnish
wholemeal bread and grated cheese,
   to serve (optional)

1 Heat the olive oil in a large saucepan, add the onions, cover and cook for 5 minutes. Add the carrots, parsnips, leeks, cabbage, thyme and bay leaves and stir to lightly coat them all with the oil. Cover and cook gently for a further 10 minutes.

2 Add the beans and stock, bring to the boil, then reduce the heat, cover and leave to simmer over a gentle heat for 30 minutes. Season with salt and pepper, then ladle into warmed bowls and top each with a scattering of chopped parsley. Serve with wholemeal bread and grated cheese, if liked.

Creamy fennel soup with gremolata

SERVES 4
PREPARATION 15 MINUTES
COOKING 20 MINUTES

2 large fennel bulbs, trimmed
   and sliced
1 onion, roughly chopped
900 ml (1½ pints) vegetable stock
6 tablespoons double cream
salt and pepper

FOR THE GREMOLATA

2 tablespoons chopped parsley
thinly pared or finely grated rind
   of ½ lemon
1 garlic clove, finely chopped

1 Put the fennel and onion into a saucepan with the stock. Bring to the boil, then reduce the heat and gently simmer for 15–20 minutes, until very tender.

2 To make the gremolata, mix all the ingredients in a bowl and set aside.

3 Pureé the fennel mixture in a food processor or using a stick blender until smooth. If you prefer an even smoother texture, pass the soup through a sieve into a clean pan.

4 Add the cream to the soup and season with salt and pepper, then ladle into warmed bowls and top each with a spoonful of gremolata.

Butternut squash & orange soup with nutmeg •

SERVES 4
PREPARATION 15 MINUTES
COOKING 35 MINUTES

1 butternut squash, halved
  and deseeded
2 tablespoons olive oil, plus extra
  for greasing
2 onions, chopped
2 garlic cloves, chopped
juice and grated rind of 1 orange
¼ teaspoon ground nutmeg
900 ml (1½ pints) water
salt and pepper
chopped parsley, to garnish

1 Put the squash, cut-side down, on a lightly oiled baking sheet and bake in a preheated oven, 200°C (400°F), Gas Mark 6, for 30 minutes, or until tender.

2 Meanwhile, heat the olive oil in a large, heavy-based saucepan, add the onions, cover and cook over a gentle heat for about 10 minutes, until tender. Stir in the garlic and cook for a minute or two longer.

3 Scoop out the flesh from the butternut squash halves and mix with the onions and garlic, orange juice and rind, nutmeg and some salt and pepper. Purée using a stick blender or food processor, adding a little of the water if necessary.

4 Tip the mixture into a saucepan with enough of the water to make a creamy consistency and heat gently.

5 Ladle the soup into warmed bowls and serve garnished with chopped parsley.

Iced beetroot soup

This soup, which you can also serve hot if you prefer, brought me a marriage proposal. It's particularly effective served in bowls sitting in outer bowls of crushed ice.

SERVES 6
PREPARATION 25 MINUTES, PLUS
    CHILLING
COOKING 30–40 MINUTES

1 tablespoon olive oil
1 large onion, chopped
1 large potato, peeled and cut into
   small cubes
750 g (1½ lb) cooked beetroot
   (not in vinegar), roughly diced
pared rind of ½ lemon
1.5 litres (2½ pints) water or light
   vegetable stock
2 tablespoons lemon juice
salt and pepper
chives, dill or mint, to garnish
soured cream and coarsely ground
   black pepper, to serve

1 Heat the olive oil in a large saucepan, add the onion and fry for 10 minutes, until soft but not brown, then add the potato, cover and cook gently for a further 5 minutes.

2 Add the beetroot, lemon rind and water or stock. Bring to the boil, then reduce the heat, cover and simmer for 15–20 minutes, or until the potato is soft.

3 Purée the mixture in a food processor or blender until perfectly smooth. If you prefer an even smoother texture, pass the mixture through a sieve into a large bowl.

4 Add the lemon juice and season with salt and pepper to taste. Chill until required, then taste and adjust the seasoning if necessary.

5 To serve, ladle the soup into chilled bowls and top with a spoonful of soured cream, some coarsely ground black pepper and herbs of your choice.

Chilled melon soup with mint granita ⓥ

SERVES 4
PREPARATION 20 MINUTES, PLUS
  CHILLING AND FREEZING
COOKING 5 MINUTES

1 ripe ogen melon
caster sugar, to taste

FOR THE MINT GRANITA

125 g (4 oz) caster sugar
large bunch of mint
300 ml (½ pint) water
1 tablespoon lemon juice

1 Remove the skin and seeds from the melon and cut the flesh into chunks. Purée in a food processor until very smooth. Taste and add a little sugar if necessary, then chill.

2 To make the granita, put the sugar, mint and water into a saucepan and heat gently until the sugar has dissolved, then bring to the boil. Remove from the heat, cover and leave until cold.

3 Once cold, remove the mint and squeeze it to extract all the liquid. Save about a dozen leaves and discard the rest. Purée the liquid with the reserved leaves and add the lemon juice. Pour into a suitable container for freezing, put into the freezer and leave until firm. Remove from the freezer 20–30 minutes before you want to serve it to allow the granita to soften a little.

4 To serve, ladle the melon soup into chilled bowls. Beat the frozen mint mixture with a fork (or whiz chunks briefly in a food processor) and add a scoop to each bowl. Serve at once.

Hot pomegranate & pecan leafy salad ⓥ

SERVES 4
PREPARATION 10 MINUTES
COOKING 12 MINUTES

100 g (3½ oz) pecan nuts,
   roughly broken
1 tablespoon balsamic vinegar
2 tablespoons olive oil
250 g (8 oz) peppery leaves, such
   as rocket or watercress
1 pomegranate
salt and pepper

1 Spread the pecan nuts out on a baking sheet and place in a preheated oven, 180°C (350°F), Gas Mark 4, for about 12 minutes, or until lightly browned and aromatic. Remove from the oven and tip on to a plate to prevent them from burning.

2 Mix the balsamic vinegar, olive oil and some salt and pepper in a large salad bowl to make a dressing.

3 Put the salad leaves on top of the dressing, but don't toss them. Cut the pomegranate in half and bend back the skin – as if you were turning it inside out – to make the seeds pop out. Add the seeds to the leaves, along with the pecans.

4 Toss the salad and serve immediately.

Wakame, cucumber & spring onion salad with rice vinegar ⓥ

SERVES 4
PREPARATION 10 MINUTES, PLUS
    SOAKING

5 g (¼ oz) wakame seaweed
½ cucumber, peeled and shredded
6 spring onions, chopped
1 tablespoon rice vinegar
1 tablespoon mirin (or a dash of honey
    for non-vegans)
1 tablespoon shoyu or tamari
sugar, to taste
a few toasted sesame seeds
salt and pepper

1 Put the wakame into a bowl, cover with boiling water and leave to soak for 10 minutes, then drain and chop or snip.

2 Put the cucumber and spring onions into a bowl. Add the wakame, rice vinegar, mirin or honey and the shoyu or tamari, mix gently and season with salt, pepper and sugar, to taste.

3 Put the salad into a shallow dish or on to individual plates and scatter with a few toasted sesame seeds. Serve at once.

Rocket, avocado & pine nut salad

Some fresh, warm walnut or rye bread will make the perfect accompaniment for this summer salad.

SERVES 4
PREPARATION 10 MINUTES

1 tablespoon balsamic vinegar
2 tablespoons olive oil
8 sun-dried tomatoes, chopped
50 g (2 oz) raisins
250 g (8 oz) rocket
250 g (8 oz) vegetarian Pecorino
cheese or Parmesan-style cheese,
shaved or thinly sliced
25 g (1 oz) pine nuts, lightly toasted
1 large avocado, peeled, stoned and cut
into chunks
pepper
warm crusty bread, to serve

1 Put the balsamic vinegar, olive oil and pepper to taste into a large serving bowl and beat together with a spoon until combined.

2 Add the tomatoes, raisins, rocket, Pecorino, pine nuts and avocado and toss everything together. Serve with warmed bread.

Quinoa & red grape salad
with honey dressing & toasted almonds

SERVES 4
PREPARATION 15 MINUTES
COOKING 20 MINUTES

175 g (6 oz) quinoa
450 ml (¾ pint) water
2 tablespoons flaked almonds
250 g (8 oz) seedless red grapes, halved
3–4 spring onions, chopped
4 teaspoons clear honey
4 teaspoons cider vinegar
salt and pepper
little gem lettuce leaves, to serve

1 Put the quinoa into a saucepan with the water. Bring to the boil, then reduce the heat, cover and cook gently for 15 minutes, until the quinoa is tender. Remove from the heat and leave to stand, covered, for a few more minutes, or until cold.

2 Spread the flaked almonds out on a grill pan or shallow roasting tin that will fit under the grill. Cook under a preheated hot grill for a minute or so until they turn golden. Give them a stir if necessary so they cook evenly, but watch them like a hawk as they burn very easily. As soon as they're done, remove them from the grill and transfer to a plate, to ensure they don't go on cooking in the residual heat.

3 Put the quinoa into a bowl with the grapes, spring onions, honey, cider vinegar and some salt and pepper and mix gently. This can be done in advance if you like.

4 Just before serving, stir in the flaked almonds. It's especially nice if they're still slightly warm from the grill. Serve with some crunchy little gem lettuce leaves.

Lemon-glazed & seared haloumi with herb salad

The haloumi can be marinated well in advance, but cook it quickly at the last minute so that it is light and delicious.

SERVES 4
PREPARATION 10 MINUTES, PLUS
   MARINATING
COOKING 5–10 MINUTES

**2 x 250 g (8 oz) packets haloumi
   cheese, drained**
4 tablespoons lemon juice
2 tablespoons clear honey

FOR THE HERB SALAD

**250 g (8 oz) mixed baby leaves and
   herb salad**
2 tablespoons olive oil
salt and pepper

1 Cut the haloumi into slices about 5 mm (¼ inch) thick. Put them on a plate in a single layer.

2 Mix the lemon juice with the honey and pour over the haloumi, turning it to coat the slices all over. Leave to marinate for at least 1 hour.

3 When you are ready to serve, toss the leaves with the olive oil and some salt and pepper and divide between 4 plates.

4 Put the slices of haloumi into a dry frying pan over a moderate heat, reserving any liquid. Fry until golden brown, then flip them over and fry the other side. This is a very quick process as they cook fast. When cooked, pour in any liquid that was left from the marinade and let it bubble up until it has mostly evaporated and becomes a sweet glaze.

5 Arrange the slices of haloumi on top of the salad and serve at once.

Butter bean salad with sweet chilli dressing ⓥ

SERVES 4

PREPARATION 5 MINUTES

2 x 420 g (14 oz) cans butter beans,
  drained and rinsed
1 teaspoon dried crushed red peppers
2 teaspoons real maple syrup
2 tablespoons rice vinegar
2 teaspoons toasted sesame oil
2 teaspoons shoyu or tamari
2 spring onions, thinly sliced
3–4 tablespoons roughly chopped
  celery leaves
50 g (2 oz) salted peanuts, crushed
pepper

1　Put the butter beans into a bowl, add the crushed red peppers, maple syrup, rice vinegar, sesame oil, shoyu or tamari and a grinding of pepper and stir gently to mix.

2　Add the spring onions and celery leaves, then stir again. Add the crushed peanuts just before serving, so that they remain crisp.

Warm purple-sprouting broccoli caesar with toasted almonds

Use a home-made lemon mayonnaise (see page 160) or a good-quality bought one as the basis of the dressing. I pep up the flavour with Tabasco instead of Worcestershire sauce, which contains anchovy essence.

SERVES 4
PREPARATION 15 MINUTES
COOKING 4–5 MINUTES

250 g (8 oz) trimmed purple-sprouting broccoli
1 cos lettuce, outer leaves removed, or 2 lettuce hearts

FOR THE DRESSING

4 tablespoons mayonnaise
1 tablespoon lemon juice
Tabasco, to taste
6 tablespoons Parmesan-style cheese shavings
2 tablespoons toasted flaked almonds
salt and pepper

1 Cook the broccoli in a saucepan of boiling water for 4–5 minutes, or until just tender – the time will depend on the thickness of the stems. Drain.

2 Meanwhile, make the dressing. Mix together the mayonnaise, lemon juice and enough Tabasco to give it a good zing. Season with salt and pepper and stir in half the Parmesan.

3 Tear the lettuce into pieces and put into a bowl with the broccoli. Pour the dressing over and toss lightly. Top with the remaining Parmesan and the almonds and serve immediately.

Stilton & cherry salad
with cinnamon dressing

I adapted this salad from one served by Chef Robert Bruce in New Orleans. It has a very warming, festive feel.

SERVES 4

PREPARATION 10 MINUTES,
   PLUS MARINATING

50 g (2 oz) dried cherries
2 tablespoons sherry, port or other
   fortified wine
1 large lettuce, torn, or about 450 g
   (14½ oz) mixed salad leaves
50 g (2 oz) blue Stilton, crumbled
50 g (2 oz) toasted flaked almonds

FOR THE CINNAMON DRESSING

4 tablespoons olive oil
2 tablespoons raspberry vinegar
2 teaspoons caster sugar
1 teaspoon ground cinnamon
Tabasco, to taste
salt and pepper

1 Put the dried cherries into a small bowl, cover with the sherry or port and set aside to plump up – if you can leave them for a few hours, so much the better.

2 To make the dressing, whisk together the olive oil, raspberry vinegar, sugar, cinnamon and several drops of Tabasco – enough to give it a good kick – and some salt and pepper.

3 Put the lettuce or salad leaves into a bowl with the Stilton, almonds and cherries, together with any of their liquid that remains. Drizzle over the cinnamon dressing and toss gently. Serve at once.

Salad of warm artichokes & chanterelles

Provided you have a couple of large saucepans, I think it's easier to cook the artichokes whole and then remove the leaves and choke, rather than trimming them first.

SERVES 4
PREPARATION 30 MINUTES
COOKING 50 MINUTES

4 globe artichokes, stems removed
2 tablespoons olive oil
25 g (1 oz) butter
250 g (8 oz) chanterelle mushrooms
4 garlic cloves, finely chopped
squeeze of lemon juice
1 red oak-leaf lettuce
salt and pepper
chopped chives, to garnish

FOR THE VINAIGRETTE DRESSING

2 tablespoons balsamic vinegar
6 tablespoons extra virgin olive oil

1 Cook the artichokes in a saucepan of boiling water for about 45 minutes, or until a leaf will pull off easily. Drain and rinse under cold water to cool quickly. Pull off the leaves until you get to the central fluffy 'choke', then pull this off gently with your fingers under cold running water and discard. Slice the bases thickly and set aside.

2 To make the dressing, put the balsamic vinegar, olive oil and a generous seasoning of salt into a lidded jar and shake until combined.

3 Just before you want to serve the salad, heat the olive oil and butter in a frying pan, add the chanterelles and garlic and cook for a few minutes until they are tender and any liquid has been reabsorbed. Add the sliced artichoke bases and cook for 1–2 minutes to heat them through, stirring often. Season well with a squeeze of lemon juice and some salt and pepper.

4 While the mushrooms are cooking, arrange some oak-leaf lettuce leaves on 4 plates and drizzle with the dressing. Spoon the chanterelle and artichoke mixture on top and scatter with chopped chives. Serve at once.

Thai-flavoured slaw ⓥ

This salad can be made in advance if you like; the cabbage will soften in the tasty, oil-free dressing.

SERVES 4
PREPARATION 10 MINUTES
COOKING 2–3 MINUTES

½ small cabbage, about 275 g (9 oz)
small bunch of coriander,
   roughly chopped
4 spring onions, chopped
1 mild red chilli, deseeded
   and chopped
2 tablespoons rice vinegar
1 tablespoon mirin or 1 teaspoon
   clear honey
1 tablespoon sesame seeds
salt

1 Cut the cabbage in half, cut away and discard the hard inner core, then shred the cabbage finely with a sharp knife and put into a bowl.

2 To make the light dressing, add the coriander, spring onions and chilli to the bowl, then stir in the rice vinegar, mirin or honey and season with salt.

3 Toast the sesame seeds by putting them into a small dry saucepan and stirring over a moderate heat for a minute or two until they begin to turn golden brown and smell delicious, then scatter over the top of the salad.

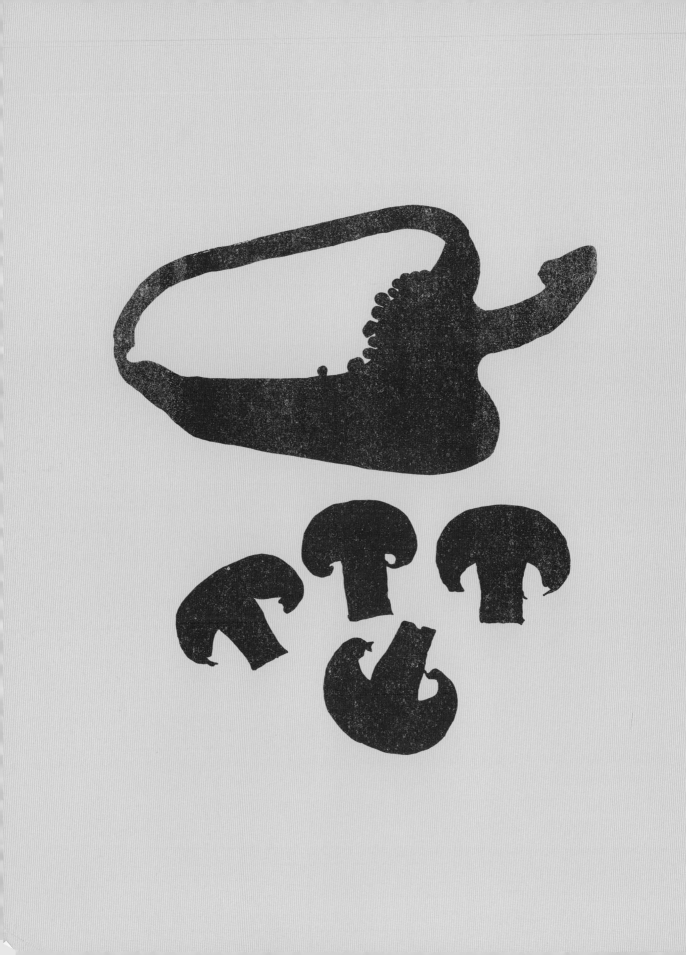

Classics with a twist

Thai-flavoured mushroom stroganoff with golden rice •

For a lighter version, use half coconut milk and half water, which is better value than buying 'light' coconut milk where you're simply paying for the water – read the ingredients on the label!

SERVES 4
PREPARATION 15 MINUTES
COOKING 20 MINUTES

1 tablespoon rapeseed oil
500 g (1 lb) baby mushrooms, halved
   or quartered depending on size
2 lemon grass stalks, crushed
4–6 lime leaves or the grated rind
   of 1 lime
1 tablespoon grated fresh root ginger
4 teaspoons cornflour
2 x 400 ml (14 fl oz) cans coconut
   milk
salt and pepper
4 tablespoons roughly chopped
   coriander leaves, to garnish

FOR THE RICE

300 g (10 oz) white basmati rice
pinch of turmeric
600 ml (1 pint) water

1 Start with the rice. Put it into a heavy-based saucepan with the turmeric, a little salt, if you like, and the water. Bring to the boil, then cover, reduce the heat and leave to cook very gently for 15 minutes, or until the rice is tender and the water has been absorbed. Fluff with a fork and keep warm, covered, until required.

2 Meanwhile, heat the rapeseed oil in a large saucepan, add the mushrooms, stir, cover and cook for about 5 minutes, or until tender.

3 Add the lemon grass, lime leaves or rind and ginger and stir over the heat for a few seconds to release the flavours.

4 Blend the cornflour to a thin paste with a little of the coconut milk and set aside. Add the remaining coconut milk to the mushrooms, bring to the boil, then reduce the heat and simmer for 5 minutes. Pour in the cornflour paste, bring to the boil and stir for a minute or so as it thickens. Season with salt and pepper, then remove the lemon grass (and, if you like, the lime leaves, if using).

5 Serve the stroganoff with the hot cooked rice topped with the coriander.

Tamari-flavoured nut roast with tomato sauce

Start this recipe by making the tomato sauce: use some of it in the nut roast mixture and serve the rest of the sauce with the cooked nut roast.

SERVES 4
PREPARATION 40 MINUTES
COOKING 1½ HOURS

1 tablespoon olive oil
1 large onion, chopped
4 garlic cloves, finely chopped
2 x 400 g (13 oz) cans chopped
   tomatoes
20 g (¾ oz) basil
125 g (4 oz) mushrooms, chopped
125 g (4 oz) soft wholemeal
   breadcrumbs
125 g (4 oz) pecan nuts, chopped
125 g (4 oz) ground almonds
1 tablespoon tamari
½ teaspoon yeast extract
1 egg
salt and pepper

1 Heat the olive oil in a large, heavy-based saucepan, add the onion, cover and cook gently for 10 minutes, stirring from time to time. Stir in the garlic and cook for a minute or two longer, then add the tomatoes. Cook, uncovered, for about 20 minutes, or until the liquid has disappeared and the mixture is very thick.

2 Meanwhile, remove one good sprig of basil for garnishing and set aside; roughly chop the rest.

3 Tip half the tomato mixture into a large bowl and add the chopped basil, mushrooms, breadcrumbs, pecan nuts, ground almonds, tamari, yeast extract and egg. Mix well and season with salt and pepper.

4 Line a 500 g (1 lb) loaf tin with a strip of nonstick baking paper to cover the base and wide sides. Spoon the mixture into the tin, smooth the surface and cover lightly with another piece of nonstick baking paper. Bake in a preheated oven, 180°C (350°F), Gas Mark 4, for 1 hour.

5 Let the nut roast stand for 3–4 minutes to settle while you reheat the remaining tomato mixture and season it with salt and pepper. You could thin it with a little water for a pouring consistency if you like, or leave it chunky.

6 Slip a knife around the edges of the nut roast, turn it out and strip off the paper. Garnish with the reserved basil sprig and serve in thick slices, accompanied by the tomato sauce.

Falafel with lemon sauce ⓥ

I generally use canned pulses for speed when cooking, but this is one recipe where you need to use dried ones for an authentic result.

SERVES 4
PREPARATION 15 MINUTES,
   PLUS SOAKING
COOKING 15 MINUTES

275 g (9 oz) dried chickpeas
1 small onion, roughly chopped
15 g (½ oz) coriander
2 garlic cloves, roughly chopped
1 tablespoon ground cumin
½ teaspoon bicarbonate of soda
1½ teaspoons salt
2 tablespoons gram flour
rapeseed oil, for shallow-frying

FOR THE LEMON SAUCE

4 tablespoons natural yogurt
   (dairy or vegan)
4 tablespoons good-quality
   mayonnaise (dairy or vegan)
grated rind of ½ lemon
1–2 tablespoons lemon juice

TO SERVE

warm halved pitta bread
shredded lettuce
sliced tomato
sliced cucumber
sliced onion
mint leaves, chopped
grated carrot (optional)

1 Put the chickpeas into a saucepan, cover with plenty of water and bring to the boil. Boil for 2 minutes, then leave to soak for 1–2 hours. (Alternatively, just soak them overnight.) Drain.

2 Put the drained chickpeas into a food processor with the onion, coriander, garlic, cumin, bicarbonate of soda and salt and whiz until the ingredients are finely ground and hold together.

3 Take a small handful of the mixture and squeeze it between your palms to extract any excess liquid. Repeat until you've used up all the mixture, then coat the falafels lightly in flour.

4 Heat a little rapeseed oil in a frying pan and fry the falafel on all sides until brown and crisp. Drain on kitchen paper.

5 To make the sauce, simply mix all the ingredients together. Serve the falafel with the warm pitta bread: people can fill the pitta halves with a selection of hot falafels, salad and lemon sauce.

No-rice nori sushi •

MAKES 16–20

PREPARATION 20 MINUTES

750 g (1½ lb) daikon or turnips,
 peeled and grated
2 teaspoons rice vinegar or
 wine vinegar
2 teaspoons sugar
4–5 pieces of nori seaweed
1 red pepper, cored, deseeded
 and cut into long strips
½ cucumber, peeled and cut
 into long strips
1 avocado, peeled, stoned and cut
 into long strips
salt and pepper
toasted sesame seeds, to garnish
 (optional)
wasabi paste and pickled ginger,
 to serve

FOR THE SOY SAUCE DIP

2 tablespoons soy sauce
2 tablespoons mirin
2 tablespoons sake

1 To make the dip, mix together the soy sauce, mirin and sake. Put into a small serving bowl and set aside.

2 Squeeze the grated daikon or turnip with your hands to extract as much moisture as possible (you need a fairly dry mixture). Mix in the vinegar and sugar and add salt and pepper to taste.

3 Place a piece of nori, shiny-side down, on a board and cover it lightly with the daikon or turnip mixture, leaving a 1 cm (½ inch) gap at the end farthest from you. Squeeze out any extra liquid, as necessary.

4 Put a row of red pepper strips on top, at the end closest to you, about 2.5 cm (1 inch) from the edge. Place a thin line of cucumber and one of avocado next to the red pepper. Fold over the end closest to you, quite firmly, then continue to roll the nori up, like a Swiss roll. Continue in the same way until all the ingredients have been used. Chill until required.

5 To serve, trim the ends of each roll – these tend to be a little untidy – then cut the rolls into 4 pieces and put them, filling-side up, on a serving plate. Sprinkle with a few sesame seeds, if liked. Serve with the soy sauce dip, a little bowl of wasabi paste and some pickled ginger.

Omelette cannelloni with spinach filling

This is delicious – an excellent dish if you're trying to lose weight, whether you're counting calories or carbs.

SERVES 4
PREPARATION 20 MINUTES
COOKING 40 MINUTES

750 g (1½ lb) spinach
125 g (4 oz) low-fat soft cream cheese
8 tablespoons grated Parmesan-style cheese
grated nutmeg
4 eggs
2 tablespoons water
1 tablespoon olive oil
salt and pepper

1 Wash the spinach, then place in a large saucepan with just the water clinging to the leaves, cover and cook for 6–7 minutes, or until tender. Drain well.

2 Add the cream cheese to the spinach along with 4 tablespoons of the Parmesan. Mix well and season with salt, pepper and grated nutmeg. Set aside.

3 Whisk the eggs with the water and salt and pepper to taste. Brush a frying pan (preferably nonstick) with a little of the olive oil and heat, then pour in enough of the egg – about 2 tablespoons – to make a small omelette. Cook for a few seconds, until it is set, then lift out on to a plate. Continue in this way until you have made about 8 small omelettes, piling them up on top of each other.

4 Spoon a little of the spinach mixture on to the edge of one of the omelettes, roll it up and place in a shallow gratin dish. Fill the remaining omelettes in the same way, until all the spinach mixture is used, placing them snugly side by side in the dish. Sprinkle with the remaining Parmesan and bake in a preheated oven, 190°C (375°F), Gas Mark 5, for about 25 minutes, or until bubbling and golden brown on top.

Vegetarian pad thai

You can buy deep-fried tofu, or make your own by cutting the tofu into cubes and deep-frying in a little rapeseed or groundnut oil for about 5 minutes, until golden brown.

SERVES 4
PREPARATION 20 MINUTES
COOKING 20 MINUTES

250 g (8 oz) rice noodles
rapeseed oil, for deep-frying
500 g (1 lb) firm tofu, drained and
   cut into 1 cm (½ inch) cubes
2 tablespoons toasted sesame oil
2 onions, chopped
4 garlic cloves, finely chopped
4 teaspoons tamarind purée
2 tablespoons soy sauce
2 teaspoons brown sugar
125 g (4 oz) bean sprouts
2 eggs, beaten
25–50 g (1–2 oz) roasted peanuts,
   lightly crushed
salt and pepper
roughly chopped coriander, to garnish
lime wedges, to serve

1 Put the noodles into a bowl, cover with boiling water and leave to soak until tender – the timing depends on the thickness of the noodles; very fine ones take 5 minutes, thicker ones take longer. Drain.

2 Heat the rapeseed oil in a wok to 180–190°C (350–375°F) or until a cube of bread browns in 30 seconds. Add the tofu and deep-fry for about 5 minutes. Drain on kitchen paper.

3 Heat all but 1 teaspoon of the sesame oil in a large saucepan, add the onions and fry for 7–10 minutes, until tender, then stir in the garlic. Cook for a few seconds, then stir in the deep-fried tofu, tamarind purée, soy sauce, brown sugar, bean sprouts and drained noodles. Cook over the heat for 2–3 minutes until the bean sprouts are tender and everything is heated through.

4 Meanwhile, heat the remaining sesame oil in a frying pan, pour in the eggs and make an omelette, pulling back the edges of the omelette as it sets and tipping the pan so that uncooked egg runs to the edges. When the omelette is set, roll it up, put it on a plate, cut into shreds and add to the noodles.

5 Season the noodle mixture to taste with salt and pepper, then serve on warmed plates and top with the crushed peanuts and a generous amount of coriander and serve with lime wedges.

Creamy cashew korma •

An electric coffee grinder is quite inexpensive and is invaluable for turning nuts into powder in an instant, and also for grinding spices – it's one of my favourite pieces of equipment.

SERVES 4
PREPARATION 20 MINUTES
COOKING 40 MINUTES

1 tablespoon rapeseed oil
1 large onion, finely chopped
2 garlic cloves, crushed
1 teaspoon turmeric
1 tablespoon ground cumin
1 tablespoon ground coriander
50 g (2 oz) cashew nuts
400 ml (14 fl oz) can coconut milk
400 ml (14 fl oz) water
small handful of fresh curry leaves
   (optional)
175 g (6 oz) okra, topped and tailed
250 g (8 oz) cauliflower florets
250 g (8 oz) broccoli florets
salt and pepper
chopped coriander leaves, to garnish
basmati rice, to serve

1 Heat the rapeseed oil in a large saucepan, add the onion, cover and cook for about 10 minutes, or until tender. Stir in the garlic, turmeric, cumin and ground coriander, and cook for a minute or two longer.

2 Grind the cashews to a powder in a coffee grinder, food processor or using the fine grater in a hand mill. Add them to the pan, along with the coconut milk.

3 For a really smooth sauce, you can now purée the whole lot in a food processor or blender (or use a stick blender in the saucepan) or, if you prefer some texture, leave it as it is.

4 Return the mixture to the pan, if you've puréed it, and add the water and curry leaves, if using. Leave to simmer for 20–30 minutes, stirring from time to time, until thickened.

5 Just before the sauce is ready, bring 5 cm (2 inches) depth of water to the boil in a large saucepan. Add the okra, cauliflower and broccoli, bring back to the boil, cover and cook for about 6 minutes, or until tender. Drain, then add the vegetables to the korma, stirring gently. Season with salt and pepper.

6 You can serve this at once, but if there's time, let it rest for a while – even overnight – for the flavours to intensify. Then gently reheat. Scatter with coriander before serving and serve with hot white basmati rice.

Oven-baked ratatouille with balsamic vinegar & caper berries ⓥ

SERVES 4
PREPARATION 10 MINUTES
COOKING 40 MINUTES

2 red onions, each sliced into 6 or 8
1 large courgette, cut into 1 cm
   (½ inch) pieces
1 large aubergine, cut into 1 cm
   (½ inch) pieces
2 red peppers, cored, deseeded and cut
   into 1cm (½ inch) pieces
2 tablespoons olive oil
1–2 tablespoons balsamic vinegar
400 g (13 oz) can chopped tomatoes
4 garlic cloves, roughly chopped
1–2 tablespoons caper berries, drained
salt and pepper

1 Put the onions, courgette, aubergine and peppers into a roasting tin with the olive oil and 1 tablespoon of the balsamic vinegar. Toss the vegetables to coat them all with the oil and vinegar, then season with salt and pepper.

2 Bake in a preheated oven, 200°C (400°F), Gas Mark 6, uncovered, for 20 minutes, then add the tomatoes, garlic and caper berries. Stir well and cook for a further 20 minutes, or until all the vegetables are tender.

3 Taste the ratatouille and add a little more balsamic vinegar and salt and pepper, if necessary. Serve hot, warm or cold.

Lentil shepherd's pie with smoky cheese mash

This is such a tasty, satisfying dish and I find it goes down very well with even the most hardened carnivores. It's convenient, too, because it can be made in advance, ready for the final cooking.

SERVES 4
PREPARATION 30 MINUTES
COOKING 1 HOUR

1.1 kg (2¼ lb) potatoes, peeled
    and cut into even-sized pieces
2 tablespoons olive oil
2 large onions, chopped
2 garlic cloves, crushed
400 g (13 oz) can chopped tomatoes
410 g (13½ oz) can green lentils,
    drained
50 g (2 oz) sun-blush tomatoes,
    chopped
1 tablespoon tomato ketchup
15 g (½ oz) butter
200 g (7 oz) smoked Wensleydale or
    Cheddar cheese, grated or crumbled
salt and pepper
cooked petits pois or kale, to serve

1 Put the potatoes into a saucepan, cover with water and bring to the boil. Boil for about 20 minutes, or until tender.

2 Meanwhile, heat the olive oil in a large saucepan, add the onions, cover and cook for 15 minutes, or until very tender, lightly browned and sweet. Remove from the heat and add the garlic, tomatoes, lentils, sun-blush tomatoes and tomato ketchup. Season with salt and pepper to taste.

3 Drain the boiled potatoes, reserving the water, then mash with the butter and enough of the reserved water to make a creamy consistency. Stir in two-thirds of the cheese.

4 Pour the lentil mixture into a shallow casserole dish and spread the potato on top. Scatter with the remaining cheese and bake in a preheated oven, 200°C (400°F), Gas Mark 6, for 40 minutes, until golden brown. Serve with petits pois or kale.

Kedgeree with eggs & tarragon butter

SERVES 4
PREPARATION 20 MINUTES
COOKING 35 MINUTES

1 tablespoon olive oil
1 large onion, chopped
3 garlic cloves, finely chopped
¼ teaspoon turmeric
300 g (10 oz) basmati rice
150 g (5 oz) split red lentils
750 ml (1¼ pints) water
2 tablespoons lemon juice
4–6 hens' eggs or 8–12 quails' eggs,
    hard-boiled and halved
salad of peppery leaves, such
    as rocket, to serve
salt and pepper

FOR THE TARRAGON BUTTER

75 g (3 oz) butter, softened
4 tablespoons chopped tarragon

1 Heat the olive oil in a large, heavy-based saucepan, add the onion, cover and cook gently for 10 minutes, stirring from time to time.

2 Stir in the garlic and turmeric and cook for a minute or two longer, then add the rice and lentils and stir until they are coated with the onion and spice mixture.

3 Pour in the water and bring to the boil, then reduce the heat, cover and leave to cook very gently for 20 minutes, until the lentils are pale, the rice tender and all the water absorbed.

4 While the rice is cooking, make the tarragon butter. Beat the butter with a fork until creamy, then stir in the tarragon. Form into a sausage shape on a piece of greaseproof paper or foil and refrigerate until required.

5 Using a fork, gently stir the lemon juice into the rice – this will brighten the colour instantly – and season with salt and pepper. Turn the mixture into a shallow warmed serving dish or on to individual plates and top with pieces of tarragon butter and the cooked eggs. Serve at once with a salad of peppery leaves, such as rocket.

Green risotto with spinach, peas, herbs & runner beans •

It's hard to believe that such a delectable risotto is actually low in fat: it's such a treat. If you want to serve an accompaniment, roasted tomatoes complement it perfectly.

SERVES 4
PREPARATION 30 MINUTES, PLUS
   STANDING
COOKING 35 MINUTES

1 tablespoon olive oil
1 onion, chopped
1 celery stick, finely chopped
125 g (4 oz) runner beans, trimmed
   and cut into 2.5 cm (1 inch) lengths
1 teaspoon vegetable stock powder
   or 1 cube
1 large garlic clove, crushed
400 g (13 oz) risotto rice
250 ml (8 fl oz) white wine
125 g (4 oz) baby leaf spinach
125 g (4 oz) fresh or frozen petits pois
3–4 tablespoons chopped herbs –
   parsley, mint, dill, chives, whatever
   is available
salt and pepper
grated or shaved Parmesan-style
   cheese, to serve (optional)

1 Heat the olive oil in a large saucepan, add the onion and celery and stir, then cover and cook for 7 minutes.

2 Meanwhile, cook the runner beans in a saucepan of boiling water for 4–5 minutes, or until just tender. Drain and set aside, reserving the liquid. Make the liquid up to 1.2 litres (2 pints) and put into a pan with the vegetable stock powder or cube. Bring to the boil, then reduce the heat and keep the stock hot over a very gentle heat.

3 Add the garlic and rice to the onion and celery in the pan and stir well. Add half the white wine and continue cooking, stirring all the time, until the wine has bubbled away. Repeat the process with the remaining wine, then add the hot stock in the same way, a ladleful at a time.

4 When the rice is tender and all or most of the stock has been used up – about 25 minutes – add the spinach, reserved beans, peas and herbs, cover and leave to stand for 5 minutes, until the spinach is cooked.

5 Season with salt and pepper and serve at once with a little Parmesan, if you like.

Tagliatelle of cabbage with cream cheese, herb & garlic sauce

SERVES 4
PREPARATION 10 MINUTES
COOKING 10 MINUTES

1 kg (2 lb) hearty pale green cabbage,
   such as 'sweetheart' or 'January
   King', hard core removed and leaves
   cut into long strands like tagliatelle
250 g (8 oz) low-fat soft cream cheese
2 garlic cloves, crushed
4 tablespoons chopped parsley
   and chives
grated rind of 1 lemon
salt and pepper
shaved or grated Parmesan-style
   cheese, to serve (optional)

1 Half-fill a large saucepan with water and bring to the boil. Add the cabbage, bring back to the boil and cook, uncovered, for 5–6 minutes, or until tender. Drain and return the cabbage to the saucepan.

2 Add the cream cheese to the pan, along with the garlic, herbs, lemon rind and some salt and pepper to taste. Mix well gently, then serve on warmed plates topped with a little Parmesan, if you like.

Mediterranean stuffed peppers
with cauliflower mash

The cauliflower mash is like a very light version of mashed potatoes but with a fraction of the calories. It's also low in carbs and a good way of getting one of the daily 'five portions' of fruit and vegetables – cauliflower counts as a portion but potatoes don't. You could also serve these peppers with cauliflower 'rice' (see page 108).

SERVES 4
PREPARATION 10 MINUTES
COOKING 30 MINUTES

4 red peppers, such as ramiro
200 g (7 oz) feta cheese, cut into
   1 cm (½ inch) cubes
8 heaped teaspoons pesto
16 cherry tomatoes, halved

FOR THE CAULIFLOWER MASH

1 cauliflower, trimmed and cut
   into florets
25 g (1 oz) butter
salt and pepper

1 Halve the peppers, cutting right through the stems too if you can. Trim the insides and rinse away all the seeds. Put the peppers in a roasting tin or large shallow casserole dish. Divide the feta between the peppers, then spoon over the pesto. Finally top with the tomatoes, skin-side up.

2 Bake in a preheated oven, 200°C (400°F), Gas Mark 6, for 30 minutes, or until the tops are charring and the insides full of luscious juice.

3 Meanwhile, make the cauliflower mash. Bring 5 cm (2 inches) depth of water to the boil in a large saucepan. Add the cauliflower, bring back to the boil, cover and cook for 5–6 minutes, until tender. Drain well. Put the cauliflower into a food processor with the butter and some salt and pepper and whiz to a smooth, thick mixture. Return to the saucepan and gently reheat, stirring so that it doesn't catch, then serve with the peppers.

Laksa ⓥ

You need Thai paste for this Malaysian soup/stew – most contain shrimp paste so read the label to find one that's vegetarian.

SERVES 4
PREPARATION 15 MINUTES
COOKING 20 MINUTES

125 g (4 oz) rice noodles
2 tablespoons sesame oil
1 tablespoon vegetarian Thai paste
250 g (8 oz) shiitake mushrooms, sliced
1 red chilli, deseeded and sliced
400 ml (14 fl oz) can coconut milk
600 ml (1 pint) water
1 aubergine, stem trimmed
2 pak choi, trimmed and halved
125 g (4 oz) baby sweetcorn, halved diagonally
salt and pepper
20 g (¾ oz) coriander, roughly chopped, to garnish

1 Put the noodles into a bowl, cover with boiling water and leave to soak for 5–10 minutes, until tender, then drain.

2 Heat 1 tablespoon of the sesame oil in a large saucepan, add the Thai paste and let it sizzle for a few seconds until aromatic, then stir in the mushrooms and chilli. Pour in the coconut milk and water, then reduce the heat, cover and leave to simmer for 10–15 minutes.

3 Meanwhile, cut the aubergine into 7 mm (⅓ inch) slices and brush on both sides with the remaining oil. Place in a grill pan and cook under a preheated grill until tender and lightly browned – about 7 minutes on each side. Leave to cool, then cut into dice.

4 Cook the pak choi in a saucepan of boiling water for about 6 minutes, or until tender. Drain well.

5 Add the noodles, aubergine, pak choi and sweetcorn to the coconut mixture. Bring to the boil and simmer gently for a minute or two, to heat everything through and cook the sweetcorn.

6 Season with salt and pepper as necessary, ladle into warmed bowls and top each with some coriander to garnish.

Stir-fry with sizzling tofu ⓥ

A fine microplane grater revolutionizes garlic crushing; just grate the garlic, skin and all, for perfect results. (It also works for fresh root ginger – there is no need to peel it first.) Immerse the grater in water immediately after use to make cleaning easier.

SERVES 6

PREPARATION 15 MINUTES,
   PLUS MARINATING

COOKING 15 MINUTES

1 tablespoon sesame oil
2 teaspoons vegetarian Thai red curry
   paste
2 garlic cloves, crushed
2 teaspoons grated fresh root ginger
300 g (10 oz) bean sprouts
1 red pepper, cored, deseeded and
   thinly sliced
bunch of spring onions, trimmed
   and chopped
125 g (4 oz) button mushrooms
150 g (5 oz) mangetout, halved
   lengthways
1 tablespoon soy sauce
coriander leaves, to garnish
salt

FOR THE TOFU

1 tablespoon grated fresh root ginger
4 garlic cloves, crushed
1 teaspoon brown sugar
1 teaspoon Dijon mustard
4 tablespoons soy sauce
500 g (1 lb) firm tofu, drained and cut
   into 5 mm (¼ inch) slices
very light olive oil, for shallow-frying

1 Start with the tofu. Put the ginger, garlic, sugar, mustard and soy sauce into a shallow dish and mix together. Toss the pieces of tofu in this mixture until they are well coated. Leave to marinate for as long as you can – 10–30 minutes or up to 24 hours.

2 To make the stir-fry, heat the sesame oil in a wok until smoking hot. Add the curry paste and stir for a few seconds over the heat, then add the garlic and ginger, and stir again. Add all the vegetables to the wok and stir-fry for 1–2 minutes, then cover and leave to cook for 5 minutes, or until the vegetables are tender. Stir in the soy sauce.

3 Meanwhile, drain the tofu, saving any remaining marinade. Heat a little hot olive oil in a frying pan and fry the tofu on both sides. You will probably have to cook in 2 batches so keep the first batch hot under a preheated grill.

4 Add any reserved marinade to the vegetables. Check the seasoning and add some salt if necessary, then serve with the sizzling hot tofu and garnish with coriander.

Three-bean chilli with multi-coloured peppers ⓥ

SERVES 4
PREPARATION 20 MINUTES
COOKING 30–35 MINUTES

1 tablespoon olive oil
1 onion, chopped
2 garlic cloves, finely chopped
1 green chilli, deseeded and chopped
1 red, 1 yellow and 1 green pepper,
  all cored, deseeded and chopped
410 g (13½ oz) can borlotti beans
410 g (13½ oz) can red kidney beans
410 g (13½ oz) can pinto beans
400 g (13 oz) can chopped tomatoes
salt and pepper
Tabasco, to taste (optional)

1 Heat the olive oil in a large saucepan, add the onion, cover and fry without browning for 5 minutes. Add the garlic, chilli and peppers, stir, then cover and fry for a further 15–20 minutes, or until the peppers are tender.

2 Add all the beans, together with their liquid, and the tomatoes. Stir and bring to a simmer, then cook over a gentle heat for about 10 minutes, until the vegetables are very tender.

3 Taste and season with salt and pepper as necessary, and a dash of Tabasco if you think it needs to be a bit hotter, then serve.

Spaghetti with black olive & tomato sauce ⓥ

SERVES 4
PREPARATION 15 MINUTES
COOKING 30 MINUTES

2 tablespoons olive oil
1 onion, finely chopped
2 garlic cloves, chopped
2 x 400 g (13 oz) cans chopped
   tomatoes
250 ml (8 fl oz) red wine
400 g (13 oz) spaghetti
50–125 g (2–4 oz) Kalamata olives,
   pitted and roughly chopped
salt and pepper
Parmesan-style cheese shavings, to
   serve (optional)

1 Heat 1 tablespoon of the olive oil in a large, heavy-based saucepan, add the onion, cover and cook gently for 10 minutes, stirring from time to time. Stir in the garlic and cook for a minute or two longer.

2 Add the tomatoes and wine to the pan. Bring to the boil and leave to boil, uncovered, stirring from time to time, for 20 minutes or until thick.

3 Meanwhile, bring a large pan of water to the boil for the pasta. When it comes to a rolling boil, add the spaghetti and cook according to packet instructions.

4 Liquidize the sauce in a food processor or blender, or using a stick blender, and return it to the saucepan. Stir in the olives, season with salt and pepper and reheat.

5 Drain the spaghetti, return to the pan with the remaining olive oil and toss gently. Then either add the sauce and toss with the spaghetti, or serve the spaghetti on warmed plates and spoon the tomato and olive sauce on top. Hand round the Parmesan separately, if using.

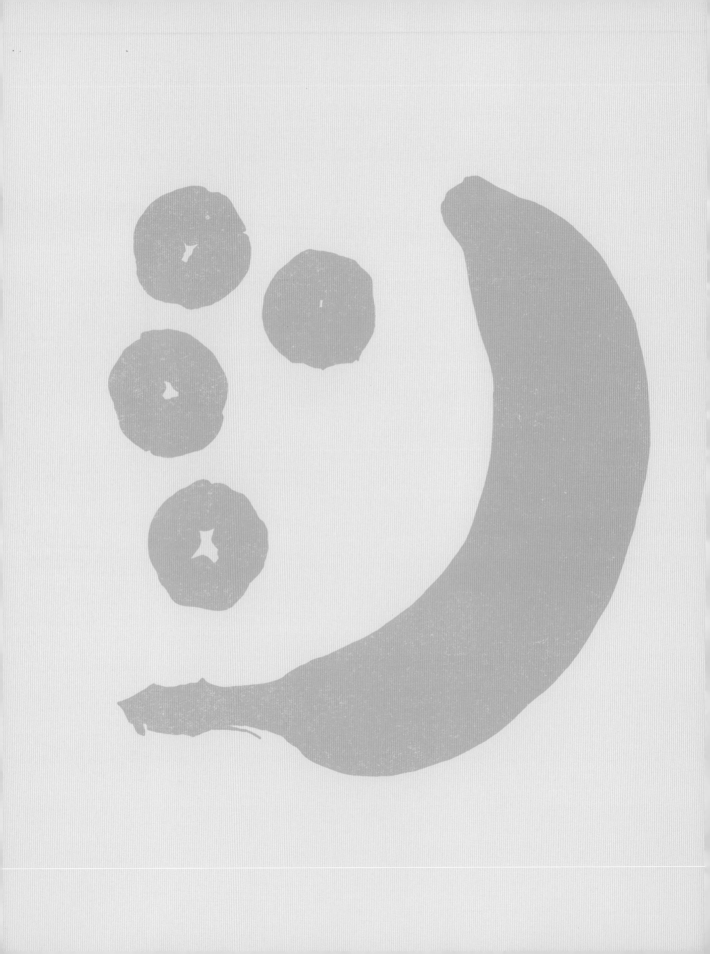

Midweek meals

Chargrilled artichoke heart & basil frittata

If you can't get chargrilled artichoke hearts, any halved artichoke hearts in oil from a jar or loose from a deli will be fine. Any frittata that's left over is wonderful cold, perhaps served with a lemon mayonnaise and a crisp green salad.

SERVES 4
PREPARATION 10 MINUTES
COOKING 15 MINUTES

2 x 290 g (9½ oz) jars chargrilled
  halved artichoke hearts in oil
225 g (7½ oz) vegetarian Gruyère
  cheese or similar cheeses such as
  Emmenthal or Gouda, grated
8 eggs, whisked
salt and pepper
handful of basil, roughly chopped
leafy salad with vinaigrette dressing
  (see page 66), to serve

1 Drain the artichoke hearts but save the oil. Heat 2 tablespoons of the oil in a 28 cm (11 inch) frying pan or in a gratin dish that will go under the grill.

2 Arrange the artichoke hearts in a single layer on the bottom of the pan or dish, sprinkle over half the cheese, then pour the eggs evenly over. Season with salt and pepper and top with the basil and the remaining cheese.

3 Set the pan over a moderate heat, cover with a lid or a plate and cook for about 5 minutes, or until the base is set and getting browned.

4 Remove the covering from the pan and put the pan under a preheated hot grill for about 10 minutes, or until the frittata has puffed up and browned, and is set in the centre. Serve at once with a leafy salad dressed with vinaigrette.

Spicy okra with red onions, mustard seeds & brown rice ⓥ

SERVES 4
PREPARATION 20 MINUTES
COOKING 25–30 MINUTES

1 tablespoon olive oil
2 red onions, sliced
4 garlic cloves, chopped
4 teaspoons ground coriander
½ teaspoon turmeric
1 teaspoon mustard seeds
500 g (1 lb) okra, trimmed and
   cut into 2.5 cm (1 inch) pieces
400 g (13 oz) can chopped tomatoes
½ teaspoon garam masala
sugar, to taste
salt and pepper
coriander leaves, to garnish

FOR THE RICE

250 g (8 oz) brown basmati rice
600 ml (1 pint) water

1 Put the rice into a heavy-based saucepan with the water. Bring to the boil, then cover, reduce the heat and cook over a very low heat for 20 minutes, until the rice is tender and all the water has been absorbed. Remove from the heat and leave to stand, still covered, until you're ready to serve.

2 Meanwhile, to make the spicy okra, heat the olive oil in a large saucepan, add the onions, cover and fry for 10–15 minutes, until tender. Add the garlic, ground coriander, turmeric and mustard seeds and stir over the heat for a few seconds, until they smell aromatic.

3 Add the okra and stir to coat with the onion and spice mixture, then add the tomatoes. Cover and leave to cook gently for 15–20 minutes, or until the okra is very tender.

4 Stir in the garam masala, taste and season with salt, pepper and a dash of sugar if necessary. Sprinkle with fresh coriander and serve with the rice.

Creamy three-cheese cauliflower with walnuts

SERVES 4
PREPARATION 15 MINUTES
COOKING 20 MINUTES

1 cauliflower, trimmed and cut into
   1 cm (½ inch) pieces
300 g (10 oz) cream cheese
1 teaspoon Dijon mustard
125 g (4 oz) blue cheese, crumbled
25 g (1 oz) walnuts, roughly chopped
50 g (2 oz) Cheddar cheese, grated
salt and pepper
watercress salad, to serve

1 Bring 5 cm (2 inches) depth of water to the boil in a saucepan. Add the cauliflower, bring back to the boil and cook for about 8 minutes, or until tender. Drain, then return the cauliflower to the pan.

2 Mix the cream cheese and mustard with the cauliflower, then stir in the blue cheese. Season with a little salt if necessary and plenty of pepper.

3 Pour the mixture into a shallow gratin dish. Scatter the walnuts on top, then cover with the Cheddar (this helps to prevent the walnuts from burning). Cook under a preheated hot grill for 10–15 minutes, or until the top is golden brown and the inside hot and bubbling. Serve at once with a watercress salad.

Chunky lentil, onion & chestnut loaf with sherry gravy ⓥ

SERVES 4
PREPARATION 20 MINUTES
COOKING 1 HOUR 20 MINUTES

125 g (4 oz) split red lentils
300 ml (½ pint) water
1 bay leaf
1 teaspoon olive oil
1 onion, chopped
3 garlic cloves, chopped
1 celery stick, chopped
2 tomatoes, chopped
240 g (8 oz) vacuum-packed whole
   peeled chestnuts, roughly chopped
1 teaspoon soy sauce
salt and pepper

FOR THE GRAVY

600 ml (1 pint) water
1 tablespoon vegetarian stock powder
3 tablespoons soy sauce
1½ tablespoons redcurrant jelly
1 tablespoon cornflour
1½ tablespoons orange juice
1½ tablespoons sherry

1 Line a 500 g (1 lb) loaf tin with a strip of nonstick baking paper to cover the base and narrow sides.

2 Put the red lentils into a saucepan with the water and bay leaf. Bring to the boil, then reduce the heat and leave to simmer gently for 15–20 minutes, or until the lentils are tender and all the water has been absorbed.

3 Meanwhile, heat the olive oil in a frying pan, add the onion and fry for 10 minutes, stirring often to prevent sticking. Remove from the heat and add to the lentils, along with the garlic, celery, tomatoes, chestnuts, soy sauce and some salt and pepper.

4 Spoon the lentil mixture into the prepared loaf tin, press down well and smooth the surface. Bake in a preheated oven, 200°C (400°F), Gas Mark 6, for 1 hour, until firm.

5 Meanwhile, make the gravy. Put the water, stock powder, soy sauce and redcurrant jelly into a saucepan and bring to the boil. Blend the cornflour with the orange juice and sherry. Stir a little of the hot liquid into the cornflour mixture, then tip this into the saucepan. Stir well, then simmer over a gentle heat until slightly thickened and season to taste with salt and pepper.

6 Loosen the edges of the lentil loaf by slipping a knife down the sides, then invert the tin over a plate and turn out the loaf. Serve in thick slices, with the gravy.

Coulibiac with soured cream sauce

This makes a lovely spring or summer meal, served with baby new potatoes and buttered baby beans or courgettes. For a special occasion it's also nice served with hollandaise sauce (see page 132).

SERVES 4
PREPARATION 20 MINUTES
COOKING 55 MINUTES

125 g (4 oz) basmati rice
1 tablespoon olive oil
25 g (1 oz) butter
1 large onion, finely chopped
175 g (6 oz) green cabbage, shredded
250 g (8 oz) baby button mushrooms, halved
3 hard-boiled eggs, roughly chopped
4 tablespoons chopped dill
2 x 350 g (11½ oz) sheets of ready-rolled puff pastry
beaten egg, to glaze
maldon sea salt flakes, for sprinkling
salt and pepper

FOR THE SAUCE
4 tablespoons chopped chives
300 ml (½ pint) soured cream

1 Bring a saucepan of water to the boil. Add the rice, bring back to the boil and boil for about 10 minutes, or until tender, then drain and set aside.

2 Meanwhile, heat the olive oil and butter in a large saucepan, add the onion, cover and cook for 5 minutes. Add the cabbage and mushrooms, stir, cover and cook for about 10 minutes, or until the cabbage is tender. Remove from the heat.

3 Add the drained rice, the eggs and dill to the onion mixture and season with salt and pepper. Leave to cool a little.

4 Put the puff pastry sheets side by side on a large baking sheet and press them lightly together where they meet, to make one large piece. Trim 4 cm (1½ inches) off the sides of the pastry.

5 Spoon the rice mixture along the centre of the piece of pastry, on top of the join. Make diagonal cuts in the pastry on each side of the rice filling and fold them alternately over the filling to create a plaited effect; trim off any excess pastry. Brush with beaten egg and sprinkle with the sea salt. Bake in a preheated oven, 200°C (400°F), Gas Mark 6, for 40 minutes, or until the coulibiac is puffy and golden brown.

6 To make the sauce, stir the chives into the soured cream and season with salt and pepper. Serve with the coulibiac.

Eggs in coconut curry sauce with cauliflower 'rice'

SERVES 4
PREPARATION 20 MINUTES
COOKING 15 MINUTES

1 tablespoon olive oil
1 small onion, finely chopped
1 small green chilli, deseeded and
    sliced
2 garlic cloves, crushed
2 teaspoons grated fresh root ginger
2 tomatoes, chopped
2 teaspoons coriander seeds
4 cardamom pods
400 ml (14 fl oz) can coconut milk
3 tablespoons chopped coriander,
    plus extra to garnish
8 hard-boiled eggs, halved

FOR THE CAULIFLOWER 'RICE'

1 cauliflower, trimmed and cut
    into florets
salt and pepper

1 Heat the olive oil in a saucepan, add the onion, cover and cook for 5 minutes. Stir in the chilli, garlic, ginger and tomatoes. Stir and cook for a further 2–3 minutes.

2 Meanwhile, crush the coriander seeds and cardamom pods using a coffee grinder or pestle and mortar and add to the onion mixture. Stir for a few seconds, then add the coconut milk and cook over a gentle heat for a further 2–3 minutes. Stir in the coriander and season with salt and pepper.

3 Gently put the hard-boiled eggs into the coconut mixture, spooning it over them, and leave, covered, over a very gentle heat for the flavours to infuse while you deal with the cauliflower.

4 Bring 5 cm (2 inches) depth of water to the boil in a large saucepan. Add the cauliflower, bring back to the boil, cover and cook for 4 minutes, until just tender. Drain well.

5 Put the cauliflower into a food processor with some salt and pepper and whiz to a grainy texture – like cooked rice. Stop before it turns to mash! Return it to the saucepan and gently reheat, stirring so that it doesn't catch. Garnish the egg curry with the remaining coriander and serve with the cauliflower 'rice'.

Sweet potato & coconut dhal with coriander ⓥ

This is delicious – and tastes even better the next day. Note that the spices are added after the lentils are tender – if you add them at the beginning, they can prevent the lentils from becoming tender, as can tomatoes or anything acidic.

SERVES 4
PREPARATION 15 MINUTES
COOKING 20 MINUTES

550 g (1 lb 2 oz) orange-fleshed sweet
   potatoes, peeled and cut into 1 cm
   (½ inch) cubes
175 g (6 oz) split red lentils
1 green chilli, deseeded and sliced
400 ml (14 fl oz) can coconut milk
450 ml (¾ pint) water
1 teaspoon grated fresh root ginger
1 teaspoon ground cinnamon
½ teaspoon turmeric
salt and pepper
chopped coriander, to garnish
cabbage, rice or cauliflower 'rice' (see
   page 108), to serve

1 Put the sweet potatoes into a saucepan with the lentils, chilli, coconut milk and water. Bring to the boil, then reduce the heat and leave to cook gently, uncovered, for 15–20 minutes, until the sweet potato and lentils are tender and the mixture looks thick.

2 Stir in the ginger, cinnamon, turmeric and some salt and pepper to taste, then cook gently for a few more minutes to blend in the flavours. Sprinkle with coriander and serve with some lightly cooked cabbage, plain-cooked rice or cauliflower 'rice'.

Banana curry with cashew rice ⓥ

I love this gentle, sweet curry and it's so quick to make. You could use 2–3 plantains in place of the bananas if you prefer but cook them for a few minutes longer.

SERVES 4
PREPARATION 25 MINUTES
COOKING 30 MINUTES

500 g (1 lb) baby potatoes, halved
2 tablespoons olive oil
1 onion, chopped
2 green peppers, cored, deseeded
  and chopped
2 teaspoons mustard seeds
½ teaspoon turmeric
1 tablespoon grated fresh root ginger
4 garlic cloves, crushed
5 g (¼ oz) or small bunch of
  curry leaves
4 large under-ripe bananas, sliced
300 ml (½ pint) water
75 g (3 oz) creamed coconut,
  cut into pieces
4 teaspoons fresh, sieved and deseeded
  tamarind (from a jar)
salt and pepper

FOR THE RICE

300 g (10 oz) basmati rice
125 g (4 oz) roasted cashew nuts,
  chopped

1 Start by cooking the rice. Bring a large saucepan of water to the boil, add the rice, bring back to the boil, then reduce the heat and leave to simmer for 15–20 minutes, or until the rice is just tender. Drain, rinse with boiling water, drain again well, then return it to the saucepan and keep warm over a gentle heat until required.

2 To make the curry, put the potatoes into a saucepan, cover with water and bring to the boil, then reduce the heat and simmer for 10–15 minutes, until just tender, then drain.

3 Meanwhile, heat the olive oil in a large, heavy-based saucepan, add the onion and peppers, cover and cook gently for 10 minutes, stirring from time to time.

4 Add the mustard seeds, stirring over the heat for a minute or two until they start to pop, then stir in the turmeric, ginger, garlic and curry leaves and cook for a minute or two longer.

5 Stir in the drained potatoes and the bananas, then add the water, coconut and tamarind paste. Bring to the boil, then reduce the heat and leave to cook gently for 5–10 minutes, until the sauce is thick and the flavours blended. Season with salt and pepper.

6 Quickly add the cashews to the rice and fork through, then serve the rice and curry together on warmed plates.

Chickpea tagine with fruity couscous •

SERVES 4
PREPARATION 15 MINUTES
COOKING 30 MINUTES

2 tablespoons olive oil
2 onions, chopped
2 garlic cloves, crushed
1 teaspoon ground ginger
1 teaspoon turmeric
½ teaspoon saffron threads
2 fennel bulbs, trimmed and quartered
1 courgette, about 250 g (8 oz),
   cut into batons
1 aubergine, about 250 g (8 oz),
   cut into 1 cm (½ inch) dice
400 g (13 oz) can tomatoes
410 g (13½ oz) can chickpeas, drained
125–250 g (4–8 oz) green olives,
   pitted
1 preserved lemon, rinsed in cold
   water and chopped, or 1 thin-
   skinned lemon, finely sliced
300 ml (½ pint) vegetable stock
salt and pepper
1 heaped tablespoon roughly chopped
   coriander, to garnish

FOR THE FRUITY COUSCOUS

375 g (12 oz) couscous
1 tablespoon olive oil
450 ml (¾ pint) water
50 g (2 oz) sultanas
50 g (2 oz) dried apricots, chopped

1 Heat the olive oil in a large, heavy-based saucepan, add the onions, cover and cook gently for 10 minutes, stirring from time to time. Stir in the garlic and cook for a minute or two longer.

2 Add the ginger, turmeric and saffron to the pan and stir, then put in the fennel, courgette and aubergine. Stir for a minute or two, then add the tomatoes, chickpeas, olives, lemon and stock. Bring to the boil, then reduce the heat, cover and leave to simmer for about 15 minutes, or until the vegetables are tender. Season with salt and pepper.

3 While the tagine is cooking, put the couscous into a saucepan with the olive oil, water, sultanas and apricots and bring to the boil. Cover and simmer for 5 minutes, then remove from the heat and leave to stand, covered, until required. Fluff with a fork, serve with the tagine and garnish with coriander.

Soft polenta with leeks & dolcelatte

SERVES 4
PREPARATION 15 MINUTES
COOKING 20 MINUTES

500 g (1 lb) trimmed leeks, sliced
  into 5 cm (2 inch) lengths
250 g (8 oz) dry polenta
250 g (8 oz) dolcelatte cheese,
  broken into pieces
salt and pepper
good-quality olive oil (optional) and
  coarsely ground black pepper, to
  serve

1 Half-fill a saucepan with water and bring to the boil. Add the leeks, bring back to the boil, cover and cook for 8–10 minutes, or until the leeks are very tender. Drain, reserving the water, and keep the leeks warm.

2 Measure the cooking water and make up to 900 ml (1½ pints) with more water, if necessary. Put this liquid into a large saucepan and heat to a boil. Sprinkle the polenta on top in a steady stream, stirring all the time with a wooden spoon. Cook for 1–2 minutes, until thick and soft, then remove from the heat.

3 Add the leeks, dolcelatte and a seasoning of salt and pepper (remembering that the cheese is very salty) to the polenta and stir gently to distribute the leeks and cheese through the mixture. Serve on to warmed plates, swirl with a little olive oil if using, and grind some coarse black pepper over the top.

Sesame-roasted tofu with satay sauce & broccoli •

SERVES 4
PREPARATION 20 MINUTES
COOKING 20 MINUTES

500 g (1 lb) firm tofu, drained
4 tablespoons soy sauce
2 tablespoons toasted sesame oil
2 tablespoons sesame seeds
2 heads of broccoli, about 350 g
  (11½ oz) each, trimmed and broken
  into florets

FOR THE SATAY SAUCE

4 heaped tablespoons peanut butter
  (plain or crunchy)
400 ml (14 fl oz) can coconut milk
  (see page 70)
2 garlic cloves, crushed
2 teaspoons grated fresh root ginger
¼–½ teaspoon dried red chilli flakes
2–3 teaspoons brown sugar
4 tablespoons chopped coriander,
  to garnish

1 Blot the tofu dry on kitchen paper and cut into thin strips about 5 mm (¼ inch) thick. Put the strips on a plate in a single layer, pour the soy sauce on top, then turn the strips so that they are all coated.

2 Heat the sesame oil in a grill pan or shallow roasting tin under a preheated hot grill. Put the tofu strips in the pan or tin in a single layer and scatter with half the sesame seeds, then immediately turn them over and coat with the remaining sesame seeds.

3 Put the pan or tin back under the grill and cook for about 10 minutes, or until the tofu is crisp and browned, then turn the pieces over and grill the other side.

4 Meanwhile, make the satay sauce. Put the peanut butter into a saucepan and gradually stir in the coconut milk to make a smooth sauce, then add the garlic, ginger and chilli. Heat gently, taste and add sugar to taste. Remove from the heat and set aside until required.

5 About 5–10 minutes before the tofu is ready, bring 1 cm (½ inch) depth of water to the boil in a large saucepan. Add the broccoli, bring back to the boil, cover and cook for 4–5 minutes, or until just tender. Drain.

6 Put some broccoli, tofu and a serving of satay sauce on each plate, scatter the sauce with some coriander, and serve.

Indonesian savoury stuffed pineapples ⊘

Ketjap manis is an Indonesian soy sauce, which is sweeter and less salty than other types. If you can't get it, just use normal soy sauce and a teaspoon of brown sugar or a dash of honey.

SERVES 4
PREPARATION 20 MINUTES
COOKING 45 MINUTES

300 g (10 oz) basmati rice
600 ml (1 pint) water
2 small pineapples with leafy tops
1 tablespoon sesame oil
1 onion, chopped
100 g (3½ oz) whole cashew nuts,
  toasted under the grill
125 g (4 oz) frozen petits pois, thawed
2–4 tablespoons ketjap manis
  (see above)
2 teaspoons brown sugar
3 tablespoons desiccated coconut,
  toasted under the grill

1 Put the rice into a saucepan with the water. Bring to the boil, then cover, reduce the heat and leave to cook gently for 15 minutes, until the rice is tender and all the water has been absorbed.

2 Halve the pineapples lengthways, cutting right down through the leaves. Cut around the inside edge of the pineapple about 5 mm (¼ inch) away from the skin and scoop out the flesh. Discard the hard core. Chop the flesh into 5 mm (¼ inch) pieces.

3 Heat the sesame oil in a saucepan, add the onion, cover and cook gently for 10 minutes, until tender. Remove from the heat and stir in 4 heaped tablespoons of the cooked rice together with the pineapple flesh, cashews, peas, ketjap manis and sugar. Taste and add a little more ketjap manis if necessary.

4 Pile the cashew mixture into the pineapple shells, heaping them up well and sprinkle the tops with the desiccated coconut. Put the stuffed pineapples into a shallow casserole dish or roasting tin and cover with foil. Bake in a preheated oven, 180°C (350°F), Gas Mark 4, for 30 minutes. After 20 minutes, put the remaining rice in a casserole dish, cover and place in the oven to reheat. Serve immediately.

Corn fritters with tomato sauce

SERVES 4
PREPARATION 15 MINUTES
COOKING 15 MINUTES

250 g (8 oz) sweetcorn kernels, freshly
  cut from the cob, frozen, or drained
  unsweetened canned
1 egg, separated
25 g (1 oz) fine wholemeal flour
rapeseed oil, for shallow-frying
salt and pepper

FOR THE TOMATO SAUCE

1 tablespoon olive oil
1 onion, finely chopped
2 garlic cloves, chopped
400 g (13 oz) can chopped tomatoes

1 First make the tomato sauce. Heat the olive oil in a saucepan, add the
   onion and fry for 7–10 minutes, until tender. Stir in the garlic, then add
   the tomatoes and simmer for about 15 minutes or until all the extra
   liquid has gone. For a smoother texture, purée in a food processor or
   blender. Season with salt and pepper and set aside.

2 To make the fritters, put the sweetcorn into a bowl with the egg yolk,
   wholemeal flour and some salt and pepper and mix well. Whisk the
   egg white in a clean, grease-proof bowl until it stands in stiff peaks, then
   gently fold into the sweetcorn mixture.

3 Heat a little rapeseed oil in a frying pan, then drop tablespoons of
   the sweetcorn mixture into the oil and fry on both sides until crisp.
   Drain on kitchen paper. Keep the first batch warm under a preheated
   grill or in a cool oven while you fry the rest, then serve with the
   tomato sauce.

Tagliatelle with creamy spinach & nutmeg sauce

SERVES 4
PREPARATION 15 MINUTES
COOKING 20 MINUTES

500 g (1 lb) tagliatelle
500 g (1 lb) spinach leaves
25 g (1 oz) butter
2 tablespoons olive oil
1 onion, finely chopped
2 garlic cloves, chopped
2 teaspoons cornflour
300 ml (½ pint) single or
   double cream
grated nutmeg
salt and pepper
grated Parmesan-style cheese,
   to serve (optional)

1 Bring a large saucepan of water to the boil for the pasta. When it comes to the boil, add the tagliatelle and cook according to packet instructions.

2 Meanwhile, wash the spinach, then place in a large saucepan with just the water clinging to the leaves and cook over a high heat for 3–4 minutes, or until tender. Drain thoroughly, reserving the water, and set the spinach aside. Make the water up to 150 ml (¼ pint).

3 Heat the butter and 1 tablespoon of the olive oil in a large, heavy-based saucepan, add the onion, cover and cook gently for 10 minutes, stirring from time to time. Stir in the garlic and cook for a minute or two longer.

4 Stir the cornflour into the saucepan, then add the spinach water and stir over the heat for a minute or two until thickened. Add the spinach and the cream, then grate in a good flavouring of nutmeg and season with salt and pepper.

5 Drain the tagliatelle and return to the pan with the remaining olive oil and toss gently. Then either add the sauce and toss with the pasta, or serve the pasta on warmed plates and spoon the spinach sauce on top. Hand round the Parmesan separately, if using.

Rosti with apple sauce ⓥ

I love this combination: crisp, irresistible rosti with a sweet apple sauce. A salad of sliced cabbage and grated carrot tossed in vinaigrette goes well with it.

SERVES 4
PREPARATION 15 MINUTES
COOKING 20 MINUTES

1.1 kg (2¼ lb) baking potatoes, scrubbed but not peeled
1 small onion
1 tablespoon chopped rosemary
4 tablespoons olive oil
salt and pepper
rosemary sprigs, to garnish

FOR THE APPLE SAUCE

500 g (1 lb) Cox apples, peeled, cored and sliced
2 tablespoons water
caster sugar, to taste

1 Grate the potatoes and onion on a medium-coarse grater, or using the grating attachment on a food processor if you have one. Mix with the rosemary and add salt and pepper to taste.

2 Heat 2 tablespoons of the olive oil in a 28 cm (11 inch) frying pan. Add the potato mixture and press down firmly. Fry for 8 minutes, or until the underside is crisp and golden. Slide the rosti out on to a plate, then invert another plate on top and turn them over. Heat the remaining oil in the pan, then slide the rosti back into the pan with the cooked side uppermost, and cook for a further 8 minutes.

3 While the rosti is cooking, make the apple sauce. Put the apples into a saucepan with the water, bring to the boil, then reduce the heat, cover and cook gently for 5–10 minutes, until the apples have collapsed. Mash lightly with a wooden spoon and sweeten to taste with caster sugar.

4 Turn the rosti out of the frying pan on to a large serving plate and garnish with a few rosemary sprigs. Serve in thick slices, with the apple sauce.

South American pinto & pumpkin casserole ⱽ

SERVES 4
PREPARATION 15 MINUTES
COOKING 15 MINUTES

500 g (1 lb) skinned and deseeded
  pumpkin, cut into 1 cm
  (½ inch) cubes
4 garlic cloves
900 ml (1½ pints) vegetable stock
1 tablespoon olive oil
2 large onions, finely chopped
2 large red peppers, cored,
  deseeded and diced
2 teaspoons dried epazote or basil
kernels cut from 1 sweetcorn cob,
  or 150 g (5 oz) frozen sweetcorn
2 x 410 g (13½ oz) cans pinto beans
2–3 tablespoons lemon juice
salt and pepper
1 tablespoon finely chopped fresh
  epazote or flat leaf parsley, to garnish
warm bread, to serve

1 Put the cubes of pumpkin into a large saucepan with the garlic and stock. Bring to the boil, then reduce the heat, cover and simmer for about 15 minutes, or until the pumpkin is very tender. Tip the contents of the pan into a food processor and whiz to a thin purée.

2 While the pumpkin is cooking, heat the olive oil in another large saucepan. Add the onions, peppers and dried epazote or basil, cover and cook over a gentle heat for 15 minutes, or until the vegetables are tender and slightly caramelized.

3 Add the pumpkin purée to the vegetables in the pan, along with the sweetcorn kernels and the pinto beans and their liquid. Stir over a gentle heat until hot, then add the lemon juice and salt and pepper to taste.

4 Ladle into warmed bowls, sprinkle with fresh epazote or parsley and serve with warm country bread (I love a dark wholemeal or walnut bread with this – not very South American, but very good!).

Squash stuffed with Moroccan rice

Mini squash can be used, but they need to be large enough to be baked in halves and then stuffed, because that way they cook really well.

SERVES 4
PREPARATION 20 MINUTES
COOKING 30 MINUTES

2 small squash
1 garlic clove, crushed
olive oil, for greasing
salt

FOR THE RICE FILLING

175 g (6 oz) white basmati rice
25 g (1 oz) raisins
15 g (½ oz) butter
1½ teaspoons ras el hanout
   (see page 295)
½ teaspoon turmeric
2 tablespoons lemon juice
8 green queen olives, pitted and
   chopped
20 g (¾ oz) coriander, chopped

1 Cut the squash in half through their stems. Scoop out the seeds, then rub the cut surfaces of the squash with garlic and salt. Place cut-side down on a well-oiled baking sheet and bake in a preheated oven, 200°C (400°F), Gas Mark 6, for 30 minutes, or until the squash can easily be pierced with the point of a knife.

2 Meanwhile, make the rice filling. Bring half a saucepan of water to the boil, add the rice and bring back to the boil, then reduce the heat and simmer, uncovered, for 8–10 minutes, or until the rice is tender but still has some resistance.

3 Plump the raisins by soaking them in boiling water for 2–3 minutes.

4 Drain the rice. Reserve a couple of tablespoons for decoration. Return the rest to the pan with the butter, ras el hanout, turmeric and lemon juice and mix well. Drain the raisins and add to the rice, along with the chopped olives and coriander. Taste and season with salt.

5 Turn the squash so that they are cavity-side uppermost, then fill the cavities with the rice mixture, heaping it up. Serve immediately, or cover with foil and keep warm in the oven for a few minutes before serving.

Whole baked Brie in filo with apricot sauce

SERVES 6
PREPARATION 15 MINUTES,
   PLUS STANDING
COOKING 30–40 MINUTES

2 x 275 g (9 oz) packets filo pastry
50–75 ml (2–3 fl oz) olive oil
1 whole Brie cheese, 20–25 cm
   (8–10 inches) in diameter, firm and
   under-ripe if possible
mashed potato and green beans,
   to serve

FOR THE SAUCE

500 g (1 lb) jar apricot conserve
4 tablespoons lemon juice

1 Take a sheet of filo pastry, place on a baking sheet large enough to hold the Brie and brush the pastry with olive oil. Place another sheet overlapping it, and brush with more oil. The idea is to make a square of filo that is big enough to form a base for the Brie and that can also be brought up the sides. It's better to have too large a square than too small because you will be trimming off excess pastry later.

2 Put the Brie on top of the filo, then cut the filo, allowing about 10 cm (4 inches) all round the Brie. Now, build up more layers of filo on top of the Brie – this layer needs to cover the cheese with about 5 cm (2 inches) to spare around the sides. Fold up the bottom layer of filo to meet the top layer and roll them together to secure them and form a decorative seal all round the Brie. Brush with more oil and make a steam hole in the middle.

3 You can scrunch up some of the filo trimmings or cut ribbons out of them, brush with oil and use to decorate the top of the pie in any way that takes your fancy. The pie will keep in a cool place for several hours.

4 When you're ready to bake the Brie, place it, on its baking sheet, in a preheated oven, 200°C (400°F), Gas Mark 6, and bake for 30–40 minutes, until the pastry is golden brown and crisp. Remove from the oven and let it stand for 10–15 minutes, to settle, then slide very carefully on to a large platter. It looks fantastic, but once cut the Brie will ooze all over the place, so make sure it's on a large enough platter, preferably with sides, or on a plate standing on a tray.

5 To make the apricot sauce, put the apricot conserve and lemon juice into a small saucepan and bring to the boil. Pour into a jug to serve. Serve the mashed potato and green beans separately.

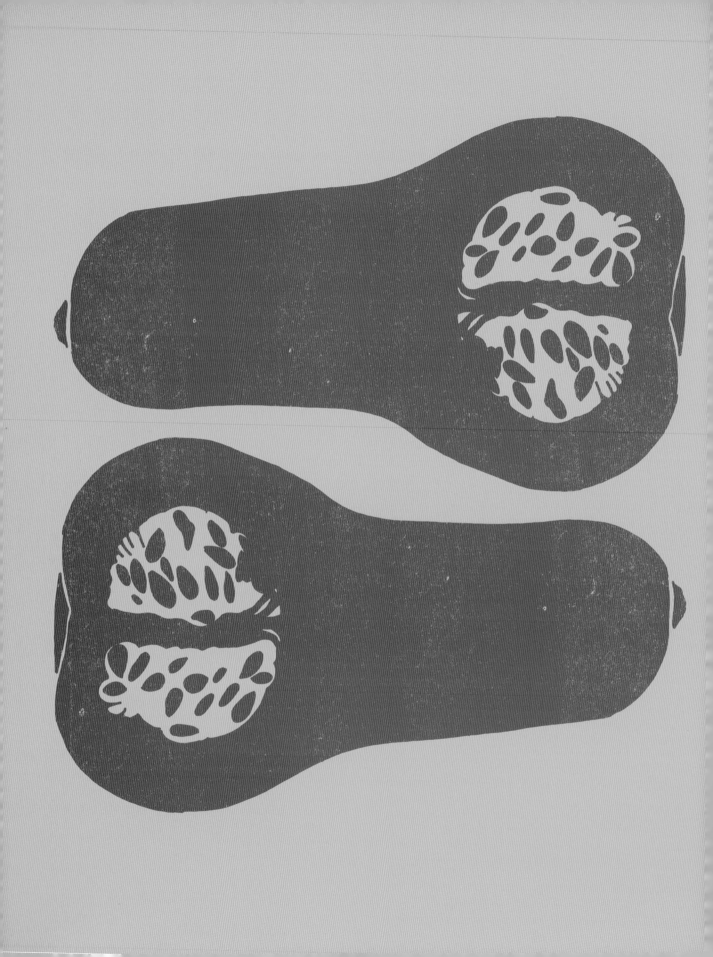

Dinners to impress

Red pepper, ricotta & fennel tortellini with tarragon sauce

SERVES 4
PREPARATION 45 MINUTES,
   PLUS RESTING
COOKING 30 MINUTES

FOR THE PASTA DOUGH

350 g (11½ oz) strong plain white
   flour, preferably '00'
pinch of salt
3 eggs
1 tablespoon olive oil

FOR THE FILLING

1 fennel bulb, trimmed
1 large red pepper, halved, cored
   and deseeded
1 garlic clove, crushed
125 g (4 oz) ricotta cheese
75 g (3 oz) Parmesan-style cheese,
   grated
salt and pepper

FOR THE TARRAGON SAUCE

100 ml (3½ fl oz) vegetable stock
   (use the fennel water)
100 ml (3½ fl oz) dry white wine
450 ml (¾ pint) double cream
2 good leafy tarragon sprigs,
   chopped

1 To make the pasta dough, put the flour, salt, eggs and olive oil into a food processor and whiz until combined. Gradually add enough cold water to make a soft, malleable dough – maybe 4–6 tablespoons. Remove from the food processor and knead on a lightly floured board for a few minutes until smooth, glossy and pliable, then put into a polythene bag and leave to rest for 1 hour.

2 Meanwhile, make the filling. Run a potato peeler down the outside of the fennel to remove any potentially stringy bits. Quarter the fennel and cook in a saucepan of boiling water until tender – 8–10 minutes. Strain – the water makes wonderful stock so save it for the sauce.

3 Grill the red pepper, cut-side down, under a hot grill for about 10 minutes, or until black and blistered in places. Cool, then strip off the skin.

4 Chop the cooked fennel and red pepper finely. Add the garlic, ricotta and Parmesan and season with salt and pepper. Divide the mixture into 20 equal portions.

5 To make the tortellini, divide the pasta dough into 20 equal portions. Take one portion and roll out on a floured board, making it as thin as you can – big enough to cut out 2 circles with a 6 cm (2½ inch) cutter. Continue with the rest of the dough, then take 2 of the circles and put a portion of filling in the centre of one. Brush the edges with cold water and place the second circle on top, pressing down the edges well. Set aside and repeat the process with the rest of the circles and filling.

6 Bring a large saucepan of water to the boil. Drop in the tortellini and cook for about 6 minutes, or until the pasta is tender.

7 Meanwhile, to make the tarragon sauce, put the stock, wine and cream into a saucepan and boil until reduced by half and slightly thickened. Remove from the heat, season and add the tarragon.

8 Drain the pasta gently in a colander, then tip it on to a warmed dish, pour over the tarragon sauce and serve.

Chestnut-stuffed onions with porcini gravy

Using polenta here instead of traditional breadcrumbs keeps the stuffing moist while preventing it from getting soggy.

SERVES 6
PREPARATION 30 MINUTES
COOKING 40–50 MINUTES

6 large onions
1 tablespoon olive oil, plus extra
   for brushing
15 g (½ oz) butter
1 celery heart, chopped
4–6 garlic cloves, finely chopped
3 x 275 g (9 oz) vacuum-packed
   whole chestnuts
1 tablespoon chopped thyme
2 tablespoons dry polenta
salt and pepper
thyme sprigs, to garnish

FOR THE GRAVY

15 g (½ oz) dried porcini mushrooms
750 ml (1¼ pints) vegetable stock
1 onion, chopped
2 tablespoons olive oil
4 garlic cloves, finely chopped
2 tablespoons fine wholemeal flour
2 tablespoons soy sauce
2 tablespoons Madeira

1 Cut the onions in half horizontally and trim them slightly if necessary to make them stand level. Using a sharp knife, cut out most of the centres, leaving about 3 good layers on the outside. Brush these onion 'cups' all over with olive oil and place in a shallow casserole dish.

2 Chop the scooped-out onion. Heat the olive oil and butter in a large saucepan, add the chopped onion, celery and garlic, cover and cook gently without browning for 10–15 minutes, or until tender. Remove from the heat.

3 Add the chestnuts to the onion mixture in the pan, mashing them a bit, then stir in the thyme and polenta and add salt and pepper to taste. Divide the mixture between the onion 'cups', heaping it up well, and bake in a preheated oven, 200°C (400°F), Gas Mark 6, for 30–35 minutes, until the onion 'cups' are tender – cover the casserole dish with foil if the stuffing seems to be drying out before this.

4 While the onions are cooking, make the gravy. Put the mushrooms into a saucepan with the stock. Bring to the boil, then cover and leave to soak for 15–20 minutes. Strain, reserving the liquid. Chop the mushrooms finely.

5 Heat the olive oil in a saucepan, add the onion and cook for 10 minutes, until tender and lightly browned. Add the chopped mushrooms and garlic, and fry for a further 1–2 minutes, then stir in the flour and cook to brown it a little. Pour in the reserved porcini liquid, the soy sauce and Madeira and stir over the heat until thickened.

6 For a really smooth sauce, you can now purée the whole lot in a food processor or blender (or strain it through a sieve) or, if you prefer some texture, leave it as it is.

7 Leave the gravy to simmer gently for 10 minutes, then add salt and pepper to taste. Serve the stuffed onions with the porcini gravy and sprigs of thyme.

Brie & cranberry soufflés

You won't need the full quantity of cranberry sauce for this, but it's not worth making less – serve the remainder with the soufflés, or keep it in a jar in the refrigerator for up to 4 weeks.

SERVES 4
PREPARATION 30 MINUTES
COOKING 40 MINUTES

FOR THE CRANBERRY SAUCE

175 g (6 oz) cranberries
125 g (4 oz) caster sugar

FOR THE SOUFFLÉS

15 g (½ oz) butter, plus extra for
  greasing
1 tablespoon plain white flour
100 ml (3½ fl oz) milk
1 teaspoon Dijon mustard
40 g (1½ oz) grated Cheddar cheese
pinch of white pepper
3 egg whites
2 egg yolks
100 g (3½ oz) Brie cheese, not
  too ripe, thinly sliced
salt

1 First make the cranberry sauce. Wash the cranberries, then place them in a saucepan with just the water clinging to them and heat gently for 10 minutes, or until soft. Add the sugar and simmer gently for about 15 minutes, or until 'jammy'. Set aside.

2 Melt the butter in a saucepan and stir in the flour. Cook for 1 minute, stirring, then remove from the heat and gradually stir in the milk. Bring to the boil and cook, stirring, until the sauce thickens, then remove from the heat and stir in the mustard, Cheddar, white pepper and a little salt. Leave to cool slightly.

3 Whisk the egg whites in a large, clean, grease-free bowl, until they stand in soft peaks. Stir the egg yolks into the cheese mixture, then stir in 1 tablespoon of the whisked whites to loosen the mixture. Gently fold in the rest of the egg whites.

4 Generously grease 4 x 150 ml (¼ pint) ramekins or individual soufflé dishes. Put 1 tablespoon of the mixture into each dish, then cover with 1–2 slices of Brie and 1–2 teaspoons of the cranberry sauce. Spoon the rest of the soufflé mixture on top – it can come to the top of the dishes but no higher.

5 Stand the dishes in a roasting tin, then pour in boiling water to come halfway up the sides of the dishes. Bake in a preheated oven, 180°C (350°F), Gas Mark 4, for 13–15 minutes, until risen and golden brown and a skewer inserted into the centre of a soufflé comes out clean. Serve at once.

Croustade of asparagus hollandaise

To save yourself a last minute rush when you're expecting guests, you can make the base in advance and refrigerate or even freeze it, either before or after baking.

SERVES 6
PREPARATION 30 MINUTES
COOKING 20–25 MINUTES

1 kg (2 lb) asparagus tips (thin if
  possible), trimmed

FOR THE CROUSTADE

150 g (5 oz) soft white breadcrumbs
150 g (5 oz) cashew nuts, finely
  ground in a coffee grinder (or use
  ground almonds)
150 g (5 oz) butter
3 garlic cloves, finely chopped
75 g (3 oz) onion, finely grated
150 g (5 oz) pine nuts
5 teaspoons water

FOR THE HOLLANDAISE SAUCE

250 g (8 oz) butter, cut into chunks
4 egg yolks
2 tablespoons lemon juice
salt and pepper

1 First make the croustade. Mix together the breadcrumbs, ground nuts, butter, garlic and onion, by hand or by whizzing in a food processor, then stir in the pine nuts and water and mix to make a dough.

2 Press the mixture down lightly into the base of a 30 cm (12 inch) shallow ovenproof or pizza dish. Bake in a preheated oven, 200°C (400°F), Gas Mark 6, for 15–20 minutes, until crisp and golden brown. Set aside.

3 Cook the asparagus in a little boiling water in a saucepan for 3–4 minutes, or until tender, then drain.

4 Meanwhile, make the sauce. Melt the butter gently in a saucepan without browning it. Put the egg yolks, lemon juice and some seasoning into a food processor or blender and whiz for 1 minute until thick. With the motor running, pour in the melted butter in a thin, steady stream – the sauce will thicken. Let it stand for a minute or two.

5 Pile the asparagus on top of the croustade, pour the sauce over and serve at once.

Aubergine schnitzels with watercress sauce ⓥ

Thick slices of grilled aubergine sandwiched with smoked tofu and arame – a delicately flavoured seaweed – give these schnitzels a gorgeous juiciness and smoky flavour, encased in a crisp crumb coating.

SERVES 4

PREPARATION 30 MINUTES, PLUS
   SOAKING

COOKING 25 MINUTES

5 g (¼ oz) arame seaweed
2 aubergines, stems trimmed
olive oil, for brushing and
   shallow-frying
220 g (7½ oz) block smoked tofu,
   drained
6 tablespoons cornflour
5 tablespoons water
25 g (1 oz) dried breadcrumbs
salt and pepper
lemon slices, to serve

FOR THE WATERCRESS SAUCE

bunch or packet of watercress
200 ml (7 fl oz) single cream or
   unsweetened soya cream
1 teaspoon cornflour

1 Put the arame into a bowl, cover with cold water and leave to soak for 10 minutes.

2 Meanwhile, cut the aubergines lengthways into 4 slices – or in half, then in half again. (Two of the slices will have skin on one side.) Brush the cut surfaces of the aubergine with olive oil, place on a grill pan and cook under a preheated hot grill until they are lightly browned and feel tender to the point of a knife, turning them over when the first side is done.

3 Drain the arame, then purée it with the tofu in a food processor or using a stick blender. Season with salt and pepper, then spread some of the mixture thickly on a slice of aubergine and press another slice on top to make a fat sandwich. Repeat with all the slices, dividing the tofu mixture evenly between them.

4 Put the cornflour into a bowl and mix in the water to make a thick coating paste. Dip each aubergine sandwich into the paste, then into the breadcrumbs, making sure it's thoroughly coated. Heat a little olive oil in a frying pan and fry the schnitzels on both sides. Drain on kitchen paper.

5 To make the watercress sauce, purée the watercress, cream and cornflour in a food processor or using a stick blender. Heat gently, stirring, until the sauce has thickened.

6 Serve the schnitzels with slices of lemon and accompanied by the watercress sauce.

Carrot, parsnip & chestnut terrine with red wine gravy

SERVES 4
PREPARATION 30 MINUTES
COOKING 1 HOUR 5 MINUTES

3 garlic cloves, chopped
50 g (2 oz) butter, softened
2 tablespoons dried breadcrumbs
2 tablespoons olive oil
2 onions, chopped
200 g (7 oz) parsnips, cut into 1 cm
    (½ inch) chunks
200 g (7 oz) carrots, sliced into rounds
200 g (7 oz) trimmed fennel, chopped
1 teaspoon caraway seeds
200 g (7 oz) vacuum pack whole
    peeled chestnuts, roughly chopped
75 g (3 oz) fine soft wholemeal
    breadcrumbs
4 tablespoons lemon juice
2 tablespoons shoyu or tamari
3 eggs, beaten
2 tablespoons chopped parsley
salt and pepper

FOR THE RED WINE GRAVY

2 onions, finely chopped
1 tablespoon olive oil
2 tablespoons plain white flour
200 ml (7 fl oz) vegetable stock
200 ml (7 fl oz) red wine
2 tablespoons shoyu or tamari
sugar, to taste

1 Line a 900 g (1 lb 13 oz) loaf tin with a strip of nonstick baking paper. Mix the garlic with the butter and use half of this to grease the lined base and sides of the tin, then coat the base and sides with half the dried breadcrumbs.

2 Heat the olive oil in a large saucepan, add the onions, parsnips, carrots and fennel, cover and cook very gently for about 20 minutes, stirring from time to time, or until all the vegetables are tender.

3 Add the caraway seeds and cook for a minute or two longer, then remove from the heat and mix in the chestnuts, soft breadcrumbs, lemon juice, shoyu or tamari, eggs, parsley and some salt and pepper.

4 Spoon the mixture into the prepared loaf tin and level the surface. Scatter the top with the rest of the dried breadcrumbs and dot with the remaining garlic butter. Bake in a preheated oven, 180°C (350°F), Gas Mark 4, for 40 minutes, until firm on top and a skewer inserted into the centre comes out clean.

5 While the loaf is cooking, make the gravy. Heat the olive oil in a frying pan, add the onions and cook for 10 minutes, until they are tender and lightly browned. Add the flour and stir over the heat for 3–4 minutes, until nut-brown – the mixture will be very dry. Stir in the stock and wine, then simmer over a moderate heat until thickened. Add the shoyu or tamari and season with salt, pepper and perhaps a touch of sugar. Serve as it is or, if you prefer smooth gravy, strain it through a sieve. Either way, add more stock if you want it thinner.

6 Serve the terrine in thick slices with the red wine gravy.

Dauphinoise roulade with red chard & dolcelatte filling

This wonderful, unusual roulade can be made in advance, ready for reheating just before serving, when it will become crisp and gorgeous. A tomato sauce, such as the one on page 20, and fine green beans go well with it.

SERVES 4
PREPARATION 40 MINUTES
COOKING 55 MINUTES

FOR THE ROULADE

olive oil, for greasing and brushing
900 g (1 lb 13 oz) potatoes,
    peeled and thinly sliced
1 garlic clove, crushed
salt and pepper
green salad, to serve

FOR THE FILLING

450 g (14½ oz) red chard, leaves
    and stems separated
175 g (6 oz) dolcelatte cheese, roughly
    chopped

1 Line a 22 x 32 cm (8½ x 12½ inch) Swiss roll tin with nonstick baking paper and brush with olive oil. Mix the potatoes with the garlic and some salt and pepper, arrange them carefully and evenly in the tin and brush with olive oil. Cover with a piece of nonstick baking paper and bake in a preheated oven, 200°C (400°F), Gas Mark 6, for 30 minutes, then remove the paper and bake for a further 5–10 minutes, until the potatoes are tender and golden brown. Cool and set aside.

2 Meanwhile, chop the chard stems, then cook in a saucepan of boiling water to soften for 5 minutes. Add the leaves, cover and cook for 7–10 minutes, until tender. Drain very well, then mix with the dolcelatte.

3 Turn out the roulade on to its covering piece of baking paper. Cover the surface with the chard mixture. Starting with one of the short edges, carefully roll up the roulade, using the paper underneath to help – it rolls up quite easily and you can be firm with it!

4 Put the roulade on a heatproof serving dish. About 15 minutes before you want to serve it, pop the roulade back into the oven, uncovered, until heated through and crisp and golden on the outside. Serve at once, with a green salad.

Pea & mint timbales with baby vegetables & Parmesan crisps

SERVES 6
PREPARATION 40 MINUTES
COOKING 1¼ HOURS

15 g (½ oz) butter, melted
1–2 tablespoons finely grated
  Parmesan-style cheese
500 g (1 lb) frozen petits pois
4 tablespoons chopped mint
150 ml (¼ pint) double cream
200 ml (7 fl oz) single cream
2 egg yolks
4 eggs
grated nutmeg
salt and pepper

FOR THE PARMESAN CRISPS

3 tablespoons finely grated
  Parmesan-style cheese

FOR THE BRAISED VEGETABLES

1 tablespoon olive oil
25 g (1 oz) butter
500 g (1 lb) baby carrots
500 g (1 lb) tiny new potatoes
250 g (8 oz) trimmed baby fennel
75 ml (3 fl oz) water
125 g (4 oz) each asparagus tips,
  sugar-snap peas and podded
  broad beans

1 Brush 6 x 150 ml (¼ pint) individual pudding basins generously with melted butter, then dust liberally with Parmesan.

2 To make the timbales, cook the peas and half the mint in a saucepan of boiling water for 2–3 minutes, or until tender. Drain, then purée in a food processor with the two lots of cream. Add the egg yolks and whole eggs and whiz again. Pour the mixture into a sieve set over a bowl and push through as much as you can – discard the residue. Season with nutmeg, salt and pepper, then pour into the prepared pudding basins.

3 Stand the pudding basins in a deep roasting tin, then pour in boiling water to come halfway up the sides of the dishes. Bake in a preheated oven, 180°C (350°F), Gas Mark 4, for 40–45 minutes, or until a skewer inserted into the centre comes out clean. Remove and set aside.

4 To make the crisps, line a baking sheet with nonstick baking paper. Put ½ tablespoon of the Parmesan on the paper and spread it into a 7 cm (3 inch) circle. Repeat to make 5 more circles of cheese. Increase the oven temperature to 200°C (400°F), Gas Mark 6, and bake for about 5 minutes, or until the Parmesan is golden brown and crisp. Leave to cool.

5 Next, cook the vegetables. Heat the olive oil and butter in a large saucepan and add the carrots, potatoes, fennel and water. Bring to the boil, then reduce the heat, cover and simmer for 15 minutes. Add the asparagus, sugar-snaps and broad beans, then simmer for a further 10 minutes, until all the vegetables are very tender. Season with salt and pepper.

6 Arrange the vegetables on warmed individual plates and scatter with the remaining chopped mint. Turn out the timbales – they will come out easily – arrange on plates and top each with a Parmesan crisp.

Tomato, pesto & mozzarella tart with walnut pastry

The reason for using tomatoes on the vine in this recipe is for flavour rather than appearance, although they do look especially attractive in this tart.

SERVES 6
PREPARATION 30 MINUTES, PLUS
    CHILLING
COOKING 1¾ HOURS

375 g (12 oz) fine wholemeal flour
    or half wholemeal, half white
175 g (6 oz) butter, cut into
    rough chunks
½ teaspoon salt
50 g (2 oz) walnuts, finely chopped
3 tablespoons cold water
2 tablespoons olive oil

FOR THE FILLING

1.1 kg (2¼ lb) baby tomatoes
    on the vine
1 tablespoon balsamic vinegar
1 red onion, sliced
1 tablespoon olive oil
4 garlic cloves, sliced
4 teaspoons pesto
150 g (5 oz) mozzarella cheese,
    drained and cut into 1 cm
    (½ inch) pieces
12 black olives, preferably Kalamata,
    pitted
salt and pepper

1 Take the tomatoes off the vine and put them into a roasting tin. Pour the balsamic vinegar over them and bake in a preheated oven, 200°C (400°F), Gas Mark 6, for 45–50 minutes, or until they are bursting and blackened in places.

2 Meanwhile, make the pastry. Put the flour, butter and salt into a food processor and whiz until the mixture resembles coarse breadcrumbs. Alternatively, put the ingredients into a bowl and rub the butter into the flour with your fingertips. Add the walnuts and water and mix to a dough.

3 Turn out the dough on to a lightly floured surface. Knead briefly, then shape into a circle and roll out to fit a 28–30 cm (11–12 inch) shallow round flan tin. Trim the edges, prick the base thoroughly all over, then chill for 30 minutes.

4 Continue with the filling: fry the onion in the olive oil for 10–15 minutes, until soft and sweet. Add the garlic and remove from the heat.

5 Bake the tart in the oven at the same temperature as for the tomatoes for 20 minutes, until the pastry is 'set' and lightly browned. A minute or two before you take it out of the oven, heat the remaining 2 tablespoons of olive oil in a small saucepan until smoking hot. As soon as the tart comes out of the oven, pour the hot olive oil all over the base – it will sizzle and almost 'fry'. This will 'waterproof' the base of the tart so that it will remain crisp.

6 Just before you want to serve the tart, put onion mixture and the roasted tomatoes into the tart case. Season with salt and pepper, remembering that both the pesto and the mozzarella are salty. Drizzle with pesto, then arrange the mozzarella and olives on top. Bake in a preheated oven, 180°C (350°F), Gas Mark 4, for 25 minutes, or until the mozzarella has melted and browned in places.

Celeriac rosti with green beans in almond butter ⓥ

SERVES 4
PREPARATION 30 MINUTES
COOKING 20 MINUTES

1 celeriac, about 800 g (1 lb 10 oz),
  peeled and grated
100 g (3½ oz) flaked almonds
2–4 tablespoons olive oil
salt and pepper

FOR THE BEANS

250 g (8 oz) slim green beans,
  lightly trimmed and cut in half
4 teaspoons roasted almond butter
  (see page 294)

1 Mix the celeriac with the almonds and some salt and pepper.

2 Heat 2 tablespoons of the olive oil in a frying pan large enough to hold 4 x 20 cm (8 inch) metal chef's rings – or you may need to use 2 frying pans. Place the rings in the frying pan or pans and fill with the celeriac mixture, dividing it evenly between them and pressing down well. Cover with a plate or lid and cook over a gentle heat for about 10 minutes, or until the underside is golden brown.

3 Using a fish slice, flip each rosti over (still in its ring) and press down the mixture so that it is touching the surface of the frying pan. Cover as before and cook the other side.

4 Meanwhile, bring 2.5 cm (1 inch) depth of water to the boil in a saucepan. Add the green beans, bring back to the boil and cook for 3–4 minutes, or until just tender. Drain, return to the pan and toss with the almond butter and some salt and pepper.

5 Place a celeriac rosti on each plate and top with green beans. Slip off the rings and serve.

Toover dhal with lime & coriander leaf dumplings

The dumplings are very British, but with the fresh Asian flavourings they seem made to go with this dish perfectly.

SERVES 4
PREPARATION 20 MINUTES
COOKING 1¼ HOURS

FOR THE DHAL

350 g (11½ oz) toover (toor) dhal (see page 296), thoroughly washed in hot water and drained
2 litres (3½ pints) water
2 tablespoons olive oil
2 whole cloves
1 cinnamon stick
1–2 dried red chillies
6 dried kaffir lime leaves
1 whole green chilli
400 g (13 oz) can chopped tomatoes
1 tablespoon garam masala
1 tablespoon lemon juice
½–1 tablespoon sugar
salt and pepper

FOR THE CORIANDER DUMPLINGS

125 g (4 oz) self-raising flour
2 teaspoons cumin seeds
20 g (¾ oz) coriander, chopped
finely grated rind of 1 lime
4 tablespoons olive oil
4 tablespoons water

1 Put the toover dhal into a large saucepan with the water and bring to the boil. Using a slotted spoon, scoop off the foam, then reduce the heat, cover and leave to cook very gently for about 1 hour, until very soft.

2 Meanwhile, heat the olive oil in a medium saucepan and add the cloves, cinnamon stick and dried chillies. Let them sizzle for about half a minute, then add the lime leaves and sizzle again. Stir in the green chilli, cook for a few more seconds, then add the tomatoes. Bring to the boil, then reduce the heat and leave to simmer, uncovered, for 15–20 minutes, or until very thick, stirring often to prevent sticking. Remove the cinnamon stick, chilli and any large pieces of lime leaf.

3 Stir the dhal to give a creamy consistency, then add the tomato mixture, garam masala, lemon juice, sugar to taste and some salt and pepper.

4 To make the dumplings, put the flour into a bowl, add all the remaining ingredients with salt to taste, and mix quickly to a soft dough. Form into 8 dumplings. Bring the dhal to a gentle boil and drop in the dumplings. Reduce the heat, cover and cook for about 15 minutes, or until the dumplings have risen to the surface and are cooked inside. Serve from the pot or carefully transfer to a warmed casserole.

Lentil cakes in citrus broth ⓥ

SERVES 4
PREPARATION 1 HOUR
COOKING 55–60 MINUTES

FOR THE LENTIL CAKES

350 g (11½ oz) Puy lentils
1 onion, roughly chopped
900 ml (1½ pints) water
20 g (¾ oz) fresh coriander,
   chopped
1 tablespoon ground coriander
juice of 1½ limes
olive oil, for shallow-frying
salt and pepper

FOR THE BROTH

600 ml (1 pint) vegetable stock
2 lemon grass stalks, crushed
green tops from a bunch of
   spring onions
3–4 kaffir lime leaves
2 garlic cloves
20 g (¾ oz) fresh coriander,
   chopped

1 Put the lentils into a saucepan with the onion and water. Bring to the boil, then reduce the heat, cover and simmer very gently for 40–45 minutes, or until the lentils are very tender and all the water has been absorbed. Add a little more water towards the end of cooking if the lentils are sticking, but make sure no water remains.

2 Mash the lentils with the fresh and ground coriander, the lime juice and some salt and pepper. Form into 12 cakes, pressing the mixture so it holds together. Heat a little olive oil in a frying pan and fry the lentil cakes on both sides until crisp and browned.

3 To make the broth, put the stock into a saucepan with the lemon grass, spring onion tops, lime leaves and garlic. Bring to the boil, then reduce the heat and simmer, uncovered, for a few minutes, until the liquid has reduced by half. Strain, discard the flavourings and return the stock to the pan with the chopped coriander.

4 Serve the lentil cakes in shallow bowls in a pool of the broth.

Tea-smoked chestnut risotto

SERVES 4
PREPARATION 20 MINUTES,
   PLUS SMOKING
COOKING 35–40 MINUTES

FOR THE TEA-SMOKED CHESTNUTS

100 g (3½ oz) uncooked rice
50 g (2 oz) dark muscovado sugar
25 g (1 oz) black tea leaves
1 tablespoon whole allspice
2 tablespoons black treacle or molasses
1 cinnamon stick
2 x 200 g (7 oz) vacuum packs whole
   peeled chestnuts

FOR THE RISOTTO

1 litre (1¾ pints) vegetable stock
1 tablespoon olive oil
2 onions, finely chopped
2 celery sticks, very finely chopped
2 garlic cloves, finely chopped
400 g (13 oz) risotto rice
100 ml (3½ fl oz) dry white wine
50 g (2 oz) butter
100 g (3½ oz) Parmesan-style cheese,
   grated
salt and pepper

1 Smoke the chestnuts an hour or so in advance. Line a wok with foil, then put in all the ingredients except the chestnuts and stir gently.

2 Arrange a rack over the wok and place the chestnuts on top. Cover with foil and cook over a medium heat for 10 minutes, then remove from the heat and leave to stand, covered, for another 10 minutes.

3 Meanwhile, make the risotto. Put the stock into a saucepan and bring to the boil, then reduce the heat and keep hot over a very gentle heat.

4 Heat the olive oil in a large saucepan, add the onions and celery and stir, then cover and cook gently for 7–8 minutes, until tender but not browned. Stir in the garlic and cook for a minute or two longer.

5 Add the rice to the pan and stir over a gentle heat for 2–3 minutes, then pour in the wine and stir all the time as it bubbles away.

6 When the wine has disappeared, add a ladleful of the hot stock. Stir over a low-to-medium heat until the rice has absorbed the stock, then add another ladleful, and continue in this way until you've used up all the stock, the rice is tender and the consistency creamy – about 15–20 minutes.

7 Stir in the butter, smoked chestnuts and half the Parmesan, season with salt and pepper and serve, scattered with the rest of the cheese.

Butternut squash with porcini & garlic stuffing & celeriac mash ⓥ

SERVES 6
PREPARATION 20 MINUTES
COOKING 45 MINUTES

45 g (scant 2 oz) dried porcini
  mushrooms
6 fat garlic cloves
4 tablespoons olive oil
2 butternut squash
salt and pepper
flat leaf parsley sprigs, to garnish

FOR THE CELERIAC MASH

750 g (1½ lb) celeriac, cut into
  even-sized pieces
500 g (1 lb) potatoes, peeled and
  cut into even-sized pieces
2 tablespoons olive oil

1 Put the porcini into a saucepan cover with water and bring to the boil. Boil for about 2 minutes, or until just tender. Drain – the liquid isn't needed for this recipe, but you could freeze it for later as it makes fantastic stock for soups and gravies.

2 Put the porcini into a food processor with the garlic, 3 tablespoons of the olive oil and a seasoning of salt and pepper and whiz to a coarse purée.

3 Cut the butternut squash in half lengthways, down through the stem. Scoop out the seeds with a teaspoon and discard. Rub the remaining olive oil and a little salt into the flesh, then fill the cavities with the porcini mixture, dividing it between all 4 of them.

4 Put the butternut squash halves, cut-side down, on to a baking sheet and bake in a preheated oven, 200°C (400°F), Gas Mark 6, for about 40 minutes, or until you can insert a sharp pointed knife easily into the skin and the flesh inside feels tender.

5 While the squash are cooking, make the celeriac mash. Put the celeriac and potatoes into a saucepan, cover with water and bring to the boil, then reduce the heat and simmer for 15–20 minutes, or until tender. Drain, reserving the liquid (this, too, makes fabulous stock). Mash or purée in a food processor with the olive oil, salt and pepper and enough of the reserved liquid to make a soft, creamy consistency.

6 To serve, carefully lift the squash off the baking sheet, making sure that the stuffing doesn't get left behind. Cut each squash half in two and place on a serving dish – they look good arranged like the rays of the sun on a large, flat, round plate – and garnish with a few parsley sprigs. Serve the celeriac mash separately.

Tagliatelle with leek & morel cream & crisp garlic

SERVES 4
PREPARATION 20 MINUTES
COOKING 30 MINUTES

400 g (13 oz) tagliatelle
2 tablespoons olive oil
4 large garlic cloves, cut into
    thin slices, to serve

FOR THE CREAM SAUCE

25 g (1 oz) butter
1 tablespoon olive oil
200 g (7 oz) morel mushrooms
    or 20 g (¾ oz) dried morels (see
    page 296), rehydrated according to
    packet instruction, roughly chopped
2 garlic cloves, crushed
600 ml (1 pint) cream – single,
    double or a mixture
250 g (8 oz) leeks, finely sliced
2 tablespoons chopped parsley
salt and pepper

1 To make the sauce, heat the butter and olive oil in a pan. Add the morels and crushed garlic and cook gently for 5–10 minutes, until any liquid they produce has boiled away. Pour in the cream and simmer, uncovered, until reduced by half.

2 Cook the leeks in a saucepan of boiling water for 3–4 minutes, then drain (the water makes tasty stock) in a sieve and rinse under cold water to preserve the colour. Drain well, then add to the cream mixture along with the parsley and some salt and pepper.

3 Bring a large pan of water to the boil for the pasta. When it comes to the boil, add the tagliatelle and cook according to the packet instructions. Drain into a colander and return to the hot saucepan with 1 tablespoon of the olive oil.

4 While the pasta is cooking, heat the remaining olive oil in a small frying pan, add the sliced garlic and fry for a few seconds until golden and crisp – be careful not to let it burn and become bitter. Set aside.

5 Add the leek and morel sauce to the pasta in the pan and serve on warmed dishes, or serve the pasta first, then spoon the sauce on top. Either way, scatter with the garlic crisps and serve immediately.

Chickpea flatcake topped with lemon- & honey-roasted vegetables

SERVES 4–6
PREPARATION 30 MINUTES
COOKING 45 MINUTES

4 tablespoons olive oil, plus extra
   for greasing
3 large onions, finely chopped
3 large garlic cloves, crushed
2 teaspoons cumin seeds
3 x 400 g (13 oz) cans chickpeas,
   drained and rinsed
salt and pepper
flat leaf parsley sprig, chopped,
   to garnish

FOR THE ROASTED VEGETABLES

900 g (1 lb 13 oz) Jerusalem
   artichokes, peeled and cut into
   2.5 cm (1 inch) chunks
450 g (14½ oz) carrots, scraped and
   cut into batons
3 tablespoons olive oil
3 tablespoons clear honey
3 tablespoons lemon juice
grated rind of 1 lemon

1 Start with the roasted vegetables. Put the artichokes and carrots into a roasting tin with the olive oil, honey, lemon juice and rind and some salt and pepper and mix gently. Roast in a preheated oven, 180°C (350°F), Gas Mark 4, for about 45 minutes, turning the vegetables from time to time.

2 Meanwhile, make the flatcake. Heat 2 tablespoons of the olive oil in a saucepan, add the onions, cover and fry gently for 10 minutes. Add the garlic and cumin seeds and cook for a further 2–3 minutes. Remove from the heat and add the chickpeas and some salt and pepper. Mash the mixture thoroughly.

3 Put the mixture into a lightly oiled 30 cm (12 inch) round loose-based flan tin and smooth the surface. Cover with foil and bake for 15 minutes, then remove the foil, pour the remaining olive oil over the top and bake for a further 5–10 minutes, until golden – but don't let it get dry. Remove from the oven. Turn the flatcake out of the tin and slide it on to a warm serving dish. Spoon the roasted vegetables on top, garnish with parsley and serve.

Stilton, apple & sage crêpes with berry sauce

SERVES 4
PREPARATION 30 MINUTES
COOKING 30 MINUTES

1 tablespoon olive oil
250 g (8 oz) shallots, chopped
375 g (12 oz) apples, peeled
   and chopped
50 g (2 oz) fine soft white
   breadcrumbs
150 g (5 oz) Stilton cheese, crumbled
1 tablespoon chopped sage
8 crêpes, made according to the
   pancake recipe on page 189, omitting
   sugar, or shop-bought crêpes
2 eggs, beaten
dry polenta, for coating
rapeseed or groundnut oil, for
   deep-frying
salt and pepper
red chard leaves, to garnish

FOR THE BLACKBERRY SAUCE

4 tablespoons blackberry jelly or jam
1 teaspoon Dijon mustard
2 tablespoons each orange and lemon
   juice
4 tablespoons port

1 Heat the olive oil in a frying pan, add the shallots and cook for 5 minutes, then add the apples, cover and cook for a further 5–10 minutes, or until the shallots and apples are tender. Remove from the heat and add the breadcrumbs, Stilton and sage, then season with salt and pepper.

2 Put a spoonful of the filling towards the edge of a crêpe. Fold the sides over it and roll up, as if wrapping a parcel. Continue until all the crêpes and filling are used. Carefully dip each crêpe in beaten egg, then into polenta, to coat completely. Put the coated crêpes on a piece of nonstick baking paper and chill until required.

3 To make the sauce, mix all the ingredients in a small saucepan and simmer over a moderate heat for 4–5 minutes, until glossy and syrupy. Pour into a jug to serve.

4 Heat the rapeseed or groundnut oil in a wok to 180–190°C (350–375°F), or until a cube of bread browns in 30 seconds. Add the crêpes and deep-fry until crisp and golden brown. Drain on kitchen paper. To serve, pour a little sauce on each plate, add 1 or 2 crêpes and garnish with a red chard leaf.

Individual pea, spinach & mint pithiviers

SERVES 4
PREPARATION 25 MINUTES
COOKING 30 MINUTES

250 g (8 oz) baby spinach leaves

200 g (7 oz) frozen petits pois, thawed

4 tablespoons chopped mint

375 g (12 oz) frozen ready-rolled
all-butter puff pastry (see page 295)

200 g (7 oz) garlic and herb cream
cheese

4 tablespoons cream, to glaze

salt and pepper

1 Wash the spinach, then place in a large saucepan with just the water clinging to the leaves and cook over a high heat for 1–2 minutes until wilted, then drain and cool. Season with salt and pepper. Mash the peas with the mint – give them a quick whiz in a food processor or with a stick blender – so they hold together a bit.

2 Lay the pastry on a board and roll to make it even thinner, then cut into 4 x 10 cm (4 inch) circles for the bases, and 4 slightly larger ones, about 17 cm (6¾ inches) (a saucer is useful for cutting round), to go over the top.

3 Place the smaller circles on a baking sheet. Put a layer of spinach on top of each circle, leaving about 1 cm (½ inch) free round the edges. Put a quarter of the garlic and herb cream cheese on top of the spinach, then heap the peas on top and around the garlic and herb cream cheese. Cover with the remaining pastry circles, pressing the edges neatly together and crimping with your fingers or the prongs of a fork. Make a hole in the centre of each and decorate the top with little cuts spiralling out from the centre, like traditional pithiviers, if you like. All this can be done in advance. When ready to cook, brush the tops with the cream.

4 Bake the pithiviers in a preheated oven, 200°C (400°F), Gas Mark 6, for about 25 minutes, or until puffed up, golden brown and crisp. Serve at once.

Sweet potato & wild rice patties with lime salsa ⓥ

I love the contrast between the bitter green leaves and the sweet patties – if you can't get cavalo nero, use kale or spinach instead.

SERVES 6
PREPARATION 30 MINUTES
COOKING 1¼ HOURS

6 sweet potatoes, about 250 g
    (8 oz) each
300 g (10 oz) mixed basmati and
    wild rice
6–8 spring onions, chopped
2 tablespoons grated fresh root ginger
8 garlic cloves, crushed
175 g (6 oz) cashew nuts, grated
dry polenta, for coating
olive oil, for shallow-frying
salt and pepper
cooked cavalo nero, kale or spinach,
    to serve

FOR THE SALSA

pared rind and chopped flesh of 1 lime
4 tablespoons chopped coriander
    leaves
1 tablespoon desiccated coconut
1 green chilli, deseeded and chopped

1 Make a cut in the sweet potatoes, to let out the steam, place them on a baking sheet and bake in a preheated oven, 230°C (450°F), Gas Mark 8, for 50–60 minutes, or until they feel tender to the point of a knife. Remove from the oven and leave to cool a little. This can be done in advance if convenient.

2 Meanwhile, cook the rice. Bring a large saucepan of water to the boil. Add the rice, bring back to the boil, then reduce the heat and leave to simmer for 15–20 minutes, or until the rice is tender. It can be a little on the soft side for this recipe. Drain into a colander, rinse under cold water, drain again thoroughly and put into a bowl.

3 Scoop the sweet potato flesh out of the skins and add to the rice, along with the spring onions, ginger, garlic and cashews. Season with salt and pepper.

4 Form the mixture into 12 flat patties and coat with polenta, then set aside until required.

5 To make the salsa, simply mix all the ingredients together and set aside.

6 Just before you want to serve the meal, pour enough olive oil into a frying pan to coat the bottom very lightly. Heat until smoking, then add some of the patties. Fry until browned and crisp on one side, then turn them over and fry the other side, adding a little more olive oil as necessary. Lift them out carefully and put on to a baking sheet lined with kitchen paper. Keep them warm in the oven while you fry the rest.

7 Bring 2.5 cm (1 inch) depth of water to the boil in a saucepan. Add the cavalo nero, kale or spinach, then bring back to the boil, cover and cook for 6–7 minutes, or until tender. Drain, then season with salt and pepper.

8 Top each patty with a little of the salsa and serve with the greens – either all spread out on a large platter, the patties on top of the greens, or on individual plates.

Tofu braised with herbs & red wine ♥

Braising tofu in traditional French style is a great way to pack it with flavour and delectable juices. It's wonderful with creamy potatoes and a lightly cooked green vegetable or salad.

SERVES 4
PREPARATION 10 MINUTES,
   PLUS MARINATING
COOKING 45 MINUTES

2 x 250 g (8 oz) blocks firm tofu,
   drained
4 tablespoons ketjap manis (see page
   294) or soy sauce
2–3 tablespoons olive oil
2 onions, sliced into rounds
2 carrots, sliced into slim batons
200 g (7 oz) turnips, diced
2 garlic cloves, finely chopped
2 tablespoons brandy
150 ml (¼ pint) red wine
450 ml (¾ pint) vegetable stock
small bunch of thyme
1 teaspoon sugar
salt and pepper
chopped parsley, to garnish

1 Cut the tofu in half, then cut each slice in half widthways, to make 8 'steaks'. Lay these on a large shallow plate or container and pour over the ketjap manis or soy sauce, turning the pieces of tofu so that they are coated all over. Leave to marinate for 30 minutes.

2 Drain the tofu, reserving the liquid. Heat 2 tablespoons of the olive oil in a large shallow frying pan or sauté pan, add the tofu and fry on both sides until well browned. Remove from the pan, add another tablespoon of olive oil, if necessary, and add the onions, carrots and turnips. Fry for 10 minutes, browning lightly.

3 Add the tofu and its reserved liquid and the garlic to the pan with the brandy, wine, stock, thyme, sugar to taste and some salt and pepper. Let the mixture simmer gently for about 30 minutes, or until all the vegetables are meltingly tender and bathed in a syrupy glaze. Serve from the pan, topped with a little chopped parsley.

Al fresco

Toasted Camembert open baguettes with shallots, thyme & redcurrants

If you prefer, use good-quality redcurrant jelly (or cranberry sauce) instead of the redcurrant mixture.

SERVES 4
PREPARATION 20 MINUTES
COOKING 30 MINUTES

2 tablespoons olive oil
250 g (8 oz) shallots, sliced
4 thyme sprigs
125 g (4 oz) redcurrants
1 tablespoon water
125 g (4 oz) caster sugar
2 short baguettes
250 g (8 oz) Camembert cheese,
    sliced with rind
leafy salad, to serve

1 Heat 1 tablespoon of the olive oil in a saucepan, add the shallots and thyme, cover and cook gently for 10–15 minutes, until tender.

2 Meanwhile, make the sauce, put the redcurrants into a saucepan with the water and cook for 2–3 minutes, until the juices run. Add the sugar, bring to the boil and simmer for 5 minutes, then remove from the heat.

3 Split each baguette lengthways, then cut each length in half, to give 8 pieces of bread in all. Scoop out most of the soft crumb – this will not be needed.

4 Place the baguettes on a grill pan. Put a layer of shallots, with the thyme sprigs if you like, into each baguette, then top with slices of Camembert. Put a little of the redcurrant mixture along the top – you won't need it all.

5 Brush the edges of each baguette with the remaining oil, then cook under a preheated grill for 5–10 minutes, or until the bread has crisped and the Camembert has melted and become golden brown in places. Serve at once, with a leafy salad.

Spicy bean cakes with lemon mayonnaise

SERVES 4
PREPARATION 20 MINUTES
COOKING 30–35 MINUTES

1 tablespoon olive oil
1 onion, finely chopped
1 red pepper, cored, deseeded
  and chopped
2 garlic cloves, finely chopped
1 teaspoon cumin seeds
¼–½ teaspoon dried red chilli flakes
2 x 410 g (13½ oz) cans black beans
  or red kidney beans, well drained
4 tablespoons roughly chopped
  coriander
50 g (2 oz) soft breadcrumbs
a little dry polenta or dried
  breadcrumbs, for coating
rapeseed or light olive oil, for
  shallow-frying
lemon wedges, to serve

FOR THE LEMON MAYONNAISE

1 egg
1 teaspoon Dijon mustard
1 tablespoon lemon juice
300 ml (½ pint) very light olive oil
  or other neutral-tasting oil
salt and pepper

1 To make the mayonnaise, put the egg, mustard, lemon juice and salt and pepper into a food processor or blender and whiz for a few seconds to blend. Then, with the motor running, very slowly pour in the oil through the hole in the top of the mixer, barely a trickle at first, increasing as the mayonnaise thickens. It will be very thick when you have added all the oil. Check the seasoning and set aside.

2 To make the bean cakes, heat the olive oil in a saucepan, add the onion, cover and fry for 5 minutes. Add the red pepper and garlic, stir, cover and cook for a further 10–15 minutes, until the vegetables are tender. Stir in the cumin seeds and chilli flakes, cook for a minute or two longer, then remove from the heat.

3 Add the beans to the onion mixture, breaking them up with a potato masher, or blitz them briefly in a food processor until they are coarsely mashed – it's nice to have some big pieces. Add the coriander, then stir in 2 tablespoons of the lemon mayonnaise and soft breadcrumbs, to make a soft mixture that holds together. Season with salt and pepper.

4 Divide the mixture into 8 equal pieces, dip into polenta or dried breadcrumbs and form into burger shapes. Heat a little rapeseed or olive oil in a frying pan and fry the bean cakes on both sides until crisp – 2–3 minutes on each side. Drain on kitchen paper, then serve with the remaining lemon mayonnaise and some lemon wedges.

Aubergine steaks with mint glaze ⓥ

So simple – and so delicious – this has become one of my favourite ways to cook aubergine.

SERVES 4
PREPARATION 10 MINUTES,
   PLUS MARINATING
COOKING 20 MINUTES

2 large aubergines, stems trimmed
juice of 1 lime
2 tablespoons toasted sesame oil
2 tablespoons clear honey or
   real maple syrup
4 tablespoons chopped mint

1   Cut each aubergine lengthways into 4 thick slices. Cut cross-hatching on both surfaces of the slices – on 2 of them you will be cutting the skin. Place the aubergine slices on a shallow tray or grill pan.

2   Mix the lime juice with the sesame oil and honey or maple syrup. Drizzle this over the surfaces of the aubergine, turning them over to drench both sides. Leave to marinate for 30 minutes, or up to 8 hours.

3   Cook the aubergine slices under a preheated hot grill or on a barbecue until browned on one side, then turn them over and cook the other side until both sides are tender and lightly browned – about 20 minutes.

4   Scatter with the chopped mint and serve at once.

Haloumi with lime vinaigrette & mint in toasted mini pitta

This is very fresh-tasting and can be prepared in advance. I find it a very useful standby for unexpected visitors because it's easy to make and packets of haloumi keep for a long time in the refrigerator.

SERVES 4
PREPARATION 10 MINUTES
COOKING 10 MINUTES

grated rind and juice of 2 limes
4 tablespoons olive oil
500 g (1 lb) haloumi cheese
8 mini pitta breads
leaves from 1 bunch of mint,
   roughly chopped
½ cucumber, thinly sliced lengthways
salt and pepper

1 First make a lime vinaigrette by whisking together the rind and juice of the limes, the olive oil and some pepper – don't add any salt at this point because the haloumi cheese may supply enough. Set aside.

2 Drain off any water from the haloumi and blot the cheese with kitchen paper if necessary. Cut the haloumi into slices about 5 mm (¼ inch) thick and put them in a single layer in a dry frying pan. Fry over a moderate-to-hot heat until they are browned on one side – this will take only a minute or two – then flip them over and cook the other side.

3 While the haloumi is cooking, toast the pitta breads under a preheated grill.

4 Remove the slices of haloumi from the pan when cooked and arrange them in a shallow serving dish. Pour over the lime vinaigrette and scatter with the mint, making sure that each slice gets coated. Serve with the toasted pitta and sliced cucumber.

Chunky smoked cheese & parsley sausages

MAKES 12
PREPARATION 10 MINUTES
COOKING 5 MINUTES

2 x 150 g (5 oz) packets Bavarian
  smoked cheese, grated
175 g (6 oz) soft wholemeal
  breadcrumbs
6 tablespoons chopped parsley
2 shallots
olive oil, for shallow-frying or
  brushing
salt and pepper
hot pepper sauce, to serve

1 Put the grated cheese, breadcrumbs, parsley, shallots and a little salt and
   pepper into a food processor and whiz to a smooth mixture that holds
   together. Form into 12 fat chunky sausages.

2 Heat a little olive oil in a frying pan and fry the sausages for 5 minutes,
   or brush all over with olive oil and cook on a barbecue, turning them so
   that they become crisp and golden brown all over.

3 Serve at once with hot pepper sauce, while they are hot and crisp on the
   outside, melting and tender within.

Sage, onion & apple sausages

You can cook these sausages under a hot grill or on a barbecue; or you can shallow-fry them if you prefer.

SERVES 4
PREPARATION 15 MINUTES
COOKING 20 MINUTES

2 tablespoons olive oil, plus extra
   for brushing
2 onions, chopped
125 g (4 oz) stale white bread,
   torn into chunks
10–12 sage leaves
125 g (4 oz) Cheddar cheese, broken
   into rough chunks
125 g (4 oz) peeled and cored sweet
   eating apple, cut into chunks
salt and pepper

1 Heat the olive oil in a frying pan, add the onions and fry for 10 minutes, until soft, then put them into a food processor with the bread, sage, Cheddar, apple and some salt and pepper to taste. Whiz until everything is chopped and starts to combine.

2 Check the seasoning, adding more salt and particularly pepper if required. Divide the mixture into 12 pieces and form each into a fat sausage shape, pressing the mixture together well.

3 Brush the 'sausages' with oil and grill, cook on a barbecue or shallow-fry them in a little oil, turning them so that they become golden brown all over. Drain on kitchen paper and eat while hot.

Grilled polenta with roasted tomatoes

You can vary the flavouring for the polenta – try using chopped, pitted black or green olives instead of the cheese or just lots of chopped thyme and oregano.

SERVES 4
PREPARATION 15 MINUTES, PLUS
 COOLING
COOKING 50 MINUTES

1.2 litres (2 pints) water
250 g (8 oz) dry polenta
125 g (4 oz) Parmesan-style cheese or
 strong Cheddar cheese, grated
olive oil, for greasing and brushing
salt and pepper

FOR THE ROASTED TOMATOES

1.1 kg (2¼ lb) tomatoes on the vine
2 tablespoons olive oil
2 tablespoons balsamic vinegar
8–10 thyme sprigs

1 To make the polenta, bring the water to the boil in a large saucepan. Add the polenta to the water in a thin steady stream, stirring all the time. Leave it to simmer for 5–10 minutes, stirring from time to time, or until it's very thick and leaves the sides of the pan.

2 Remove from the heat and stir in the Parmesan or Cheddar and season with salt and pepper to taste. Turn the mixture on to a lightly oiled baking sheet or large plate, spreading and pressing it out to a depth of 5–7 mm (¼–⅓ inch). Leave until completely cold and firm.

3 To roast the tomatoes, put them, complete with their vines, into a roasting tin. Drizzle with the olive oil and vinegar, scatter with a little salt and the thyme sprigs and place in the top of a preheated oven, 200°C (400°F), Gas Mark 6, for 40–45 minutes.

4 Just before you want to serve the meal, cut the polenta into pieces, brush lightly with olive oil and cook under a preheated grill on both sides, until crisp and lightly charred. Serve at once, with the tomatoes.

Plantain bhajis with fresh coconut chutney ⓥ

SERVES 4 (MAKES ABOUT 20 BHAJIS)
PREPARATION 20 MINUTES
COOKING 15 MINUTES

125 g (4 oz) chickpea (gram) flour
½–1 teaspoon dried red chilli flakes
½ teaspoon turmeric
2 teaspoons ground coriander
2 teaspoons ground cumin
2 teaspoons cumin seeds
150–200 ml (5–7 fl oz)
   sparkling water
rapeseed or groundnut oil, for
   shallow-frying
1 plantain, about 325 g (11 oz)
salt

FOR THE COCONUT CHUTNEY

75 g (3 oz) fresh grated coconut
   (about ¼ of a coconut)
20 g (¾ oz) fresh coriander
juice and grated rind of 1 lime
1 teaspoon black mustard seeds

1 First make the chutney. Put the grated coconut, fresh coriander and lime juice and rind into a food processor and whiz until combined. Stir in the mustard seeds and, if necessary, a little water to make a soft, creamy consistency. Set aside.

2 To make a batter, mix the chickpea flour, chilli flakes, turmeric, ground coriander, ground and whole cumin seeds and some salt with enough sparkling water to make a batter that will coat the back of the spoon.

3 When you are ready to serve the bhajis, heat 2.5 cm (1 inch) of rapeseed or groundnut oil in a frying pan. Peel the plantain and cut it diagonally into slices about 2.5 cm (1 inch) thick.

4 Dip a slice of plantain into the batter, then put into the hot oil – it should sizzle immediately. Repeat with several more slices until the frying pan is full. Turn the slices over when the underside is golden brown and crisp and cook on the other side. Drain on crumpled kitchen paper. Serve at once in batches, with the chutney – or keep the first ones warm while you fry the rest, then serve all at once, hot and crisp.

Courgette & sweetcorn cakes with chilli sauce ⍟

As these little corncakes hold together so well, you could also cook them on a barbecue instead of frying them.

SERVES 4
PREPARATION 15 MINUTES
COOKING 15 MINUTES

2 tablespoons olive oil, plus extra
  for shallow-frying
250 g (8 oz) baby sweetcorn, sliced
  into 5 mm (¼ inch) thick rounds
400 g (13 oz) coarsely grated courgette
3 garlic cloves, crushed
5 tablespoons masa harina
  (see page 295)
1 teaspoon ground cumin
1 teaspoon dried dill weed
salt and pepper
3 tablespoons chopped coriander,
  to garnish
red chilli sauce, to serve

1 Heat the 2 tablespoons of olive oil in a large saucepan, add the corn, courgette and garlic and cook gently, stirring often, for about 5 minutes until the vegetables are tender.

2 Add the masa harina, cumin, dill and some salt and pepper and stir well over the heat for 2–3 minutes, until the mixture is very thick and holds together well. Leave until cool enough to handle, then form into 5 cm (2 inch) round cakes. You should make about 12–14.

3 Heat a little olive oil in a frying pan and fry the cakes on both sides until golden brown and crisp. Drain on kitchen paper.

4 Transfer to a serving dish, scatter with the chopped coriander and serve at once with red chilli sauce for dipping.

Mexican tart with cumin pastry

This dramatic-looking tart has a hot and spicy red filling topped with eggs. To help the eggs set neatly, use very fresh eggs.

SERVES 4
PREPARATION 30 MINUTES
COOKING 1 HOUR

250 g (8 oz) white flour
2 teaspoons cumin seeds
125 g (4 oz) butter, cut into rough
   chunks, plus extra for greasing
about 4 tablespoons cold water

FOR THE FILLING

2 onions, chopped
2 green peppers, cored, deseeded
   and chopped
1 tablespoon olive oil
2 x 400 g (13 oz) cans chopped
   tomatoes
½ teaspoon dried red chilli flakes
5 very fresh eggs
salt and pepper

1 To make the pastry, put the flour and cumin seeds into a bowl, add the butter and rub in with your fingertips until the mixture resembles fine breadcrumbs. Add enough cold water – 3–4 tablespoons – to mix to a malleable dough.

2 Turn out the dough on to a lightly floured surface. Knead briefly, then roll out to fit a deep greased 30 cm (12 inch) round flan tin. Trim the edges, prick the base, then cover it with nonstick baking paper and some dried beans to weigh the pastry down.

3 Bake the tart case in a preheated oven, 200°C (400°F), Gas Mark 6, for 20 minutes, until 'set' and crisp. Remove the paper and beans and bake the flan case for a further 10 minutes until the base is crisp. Remove the case from the oven and reduce the oven temperature to 180°C (350°F), Gas Mark 4.

4 Meanwhile, make the filling. Fry the onions and green peppers in the olive oil, covered, for 5 minutes, until beginning to get tender, then add the tomatoes and chilli flakes and simmer, uncovered, over a moderate heat for 25–30 minutes, or until very thick, stirring from time to time to prevent sticking. Remove from the heat and season with salt and pepper.

5 Spoon the tomato filling evenly into the pastry case. Make a depression in the centre, for 1 of the eggs, and 4 more evenly spaced around the edge. Break the eggs into the depressions and season lightly.

6 Cover the tart with foil, return to the oven and bake for about 20 minutes, or until the eggs are set.

Potato & white truffle torte

This has a wonderful rich and seductive flavour. White truffle is fantastic in this if available, but you can also make a very good version using Porcini and White Truffle Paste. It's very rich: great with a refreshing green salad.

SERVES 4
PREPARATION 20 MINUTES
COOKING 30 MINUTES

1 kg (2 lb) potatoes, peeled and cut
    into 5 mm (¼ inch) thick slices
2 garlic cloves, crushed
40 g (1½ oz) butter, softened
50 g (2 oz) white truffle, wiped, or
    80 g (3¼ oz) jar porcini mushrooms
    in a vegetarian white truffle paste
    (see page 295)
200 g (7 oz) Parmesan-style
    cheese, grated
salt and pepper
flat leaf parsley, to garnish

1 Put the potatoes into a saucepan, cover with water and bring to the boil. Boil for about 10 minutes, or until tender but not soft. Drain.

2 Mix the garlic with the butter and use half to grease generously a 23–25 cm (9–10 inch) springform tin. Arrange a layer of potato in the tin, then grate some of the truffle over the top, or spread some truffle paste over the potatoes. Sprinkle with Parmesan and season with salt and pepper.

3 Continue these layers, seasoning with salt and pepper between each layer, until you have used all the ingredients, ending with a layer of potato and one of cheese. Dot with the remaining butter.

4 Bake in a preheated oven, 230°C (450°F), Gas Mark 8, for about 20 minutes, or until golden brown and crisp on top.

5 Remove the sides of the tin, slide the torte (on its base) on to a warmed plate, snip some parsley over the top and serve at once.

Dough ball, haloumi & olive skewers

The dough balls are quick and easy to make, but, if you prefer, use shop-bought frozen dough balls, thawed. You need 8 skewers for this recipe – if you use wooden ones soak them in cold water for 10 minutes before use to prevent them burning.

SERVES 4

PREPARATION 20 MINUTES,
    PLUS RISING

COOKING 10–15 MINUTES

2 x 250 g (8 oz) packets haloumi
    cheese, drained
24 large green olives, pitted
olive oil, for brushing

FOR THE DOUGH BALLS

250 g (8 oz) strong white bread flour
½ packet fast-action dried yeast
1 teaspoon salt
175 ml (6 fl oz) warm water
2 tablespoons olive oil

FOR THE LEMON BUTTER

juice and grated rind of ½ lemon
125 g (4 oz) butter, softened

1 To make the dough balls, put the flour into a food processor fitted with a plastic dough blade. Add the yeast, salt, water and olive oil and pulse until a dough forms, then blend for 1 minute. Leave, with the lid on, for 45 minutes, or until the dough has doubled in size.

2 Divide the dough into 24 equal pieces and roll into marble-sized balls.

3 Cut each block of haloumi into 12 cubes. Thread a dough ball on to a skewer followed by an olive and a cube of haloumi; repeat twice so that each skewer contains 3 dough balls, pieces of cheese and olives. Brush lightly with olive oil and place on a grill pan or baking sheet. When all the skewers are done, cover them with a piece of clingfilm or a clean damp cloth and leave for 50–60 minutes for the dough balls to rise.

4 These skewers can be cooked in the oven, at 200°C (400°F), Gas Mark 6, under the grill, or on a barbecue: preheat these in advance, then cook the skewers, turning them when the first side is done. They will take about 5 minutes on each side.

5 To make the lemon butter, beat the lemon juice and rind into the butter and serve with the dough ball skewers.

Eggy tomatoes with garlic & basil

SERVES 4
PREPARATION 10 MINUTES
COOKING 15 MINUTES

4 beefsteak tomatoes
2 tablespoons milk or cream
8 eggs, beaten
50 g (2 oz) butter
1 garlic clove, crushed
8 large basil leaves, shredded
salt and pepper
buttered granary toast, to serve

1 Cut the tomatoes in half horizontally and scoop out the seeds and pulp with a teaspoon. You won't need them for this recipe, but could add them to a soup or casserole – or just eat them!

2 Season the insides of the tomatoes with salt and pepper and put them, cut-side up, in a shallow gratin dish that will fit under your grill and that you can later take to the table. Cook under a preheated grill for about 10 minutes, or until tender, but not collapsed.

3 Just before the tomatoes are ready, make the scrambled eggs. Whisk the milk or cream into the beaten eggs and season with salt and pepper.

4 Cut half the butter into tiny pieces and set aside. Melt the remaining butter in a saucepan, add the garlic and cook for a few seconds, but don't let the butter or garlic brown.

5 Pour in the eggs and stir over a gentle heat until the eggs begin to thicken and scramble. As soon as this starts to happen, stir in the remaining butter and the basil and remove the pan from the heat – the eggs will continue to cook in the residual heat.

6 Spoon the scrambled egg into the tomato halves, dividing the mixture equally among them and serve immediately, with hot granary toast.

Baby potatoes & mushrooms on rosemary skewers

If you can't get baby potatoes, use ordinary 'new' ones halved; and instead of rosemary sprigs, you could use wooden skewers.

SERVES 4
PREPARATION 15 MINUTES
COOKING 25 MINUTES

18 baby potatoes
6 rosemary sprigs, 25–30 cm
    (10–12 inches) long
18 baby chestnut mushrooms
2–3 tablespoons olive oil
maldon sea salt flakes
lemon mayonnaise (see page 160),
    peanut dip (see page 22) or red
    pepper hummus (see page 30),
    to serve

1 Put the potatoes into a saucepan, cover with water and bring to the boil, then reduce the heat and simmer until the potatoes are just tender when pierced with the point of a knife – about 6–10 minutes, depending on size. Drain and cool.

2 Using your fingers, pull off most of the leaves from the rosemary, leaving about 7–10 cm (3–4 inches) at the top.

3 Thread the mushrooms and potatoes alternately on to the rosemary sprigs – they should go on easily. Brush all over with olive oil.

4 Cook the skewers on a preheated barbecue or under a preheated hot grill, keeping the leafy ends away from the heat, for about 15 minutes, until the potatoes are golden brown and the mushrooms tender. Sprinkle with sea salt and serve with lemon mayonnaise, peanut dip or red pepper hummus.

Crispy nut balls coated in polenta

The nut mixture is moulded around a piece of garlic butter, giving a gorgeous burst of flavour as you bite into each ball. They're nice served with cocktail sticks and dipped into a sauce – either mayonnaise, if you feel like something rich and creamy, or a Japanese-style soy sauce dip for a clean, savoury flavour.

MAKES 24
PREPARATION 20 MINUTES, PLUS
  COOLING
COOKING 20 MINUTES

75 g (3 oz) butter, softened
2 garlic cloves, crushed
1 small onion, finely chopped
25 g (1 oz) fine wholemeal flour
200 ml (7 fl oz) soya milk
2 teaspoons chopped oregano
50 g (2 oz) hazelnuts, finely ground
1 egg, beaten
dry polenta, for coating
rapeseed oil, for deep-frying
salt and pepper
lemon wedges, to serve

FOR THE SOY SAUCE DIP

2 tablespoons soy sauce
2 tablespoons mirin
2 tablespoons sake

1 To make the dip, mix together the soy sauce, mirin and sake. Put it into a small serving bowl and set aside.

2 Beat 50 g (2 oz) of the butter with the garlic until light and creamy, then form into a small block, wrap in foil and put into the refrigerator to chill and harden – this can be done well in advance if convenient.

3 Next, make the nut mixture, which also needs to be done in advance, so it can cool before use. Melt the remaining butter in a large saucepan, add the onion, cover and fry gently for about 7 minutes, until tender. Stir in the wholemeal flour and cook for 2–3 minutes, but don't let it brown, then pour in the soya milk and stir over the heat until very thick. Remove from the heat, stir in the oregano, ground hazelnuts and salt and pepper to taste. Spread out on a plate and leave to get completely cold.

4 Divide the firm garlic butter into 24 pieces. Take a heaped teaspoon of the nut mixture, form it into a small ball, then push a piece of garlic butter into the centre and cover over with the nut mixture. Dip into beaten egg, then into the polenta. Continue until you've used all the butter and nut mixture and made 24 balls.

5 Heat the rapeseed oil in a wok to 180°C (350°F), or until a cube of bread browns in 30 seconds. Add the nut balls, a few at a time, and deep-fry for a minute or two until golden brown and crisp. Drain on kitchen paper.

6 Put the nut balls on a serving plate and serve with the bowl of soy sauce dip, or just as they are with cocktail sticks, mayonnaise and lemon wedges.

Cheese & sun-blush tomato muffins

Everyone enjoys these light, puffy, protein-rich savoury muffins – and as they don't contain any wheat flour, they're ideal for people who are watching their carbohydrate intake.

MAKES 9
PREPARATION 10 MINUTES
COOKING 20 MINUTES

225 g (7½ oz) plain cottage cheese
65 g (2½ oz) Parmesan-style cheese, grated
50 g (2 oz) soya flour
100 g (3½ oz) ground almonds
1 teaspoon baking powder
8 sun-blush tomato pieces, finely chopped
4 tablespoons chopped basil
4 tablespoons water
4 eggs
salt and pepper

1 Line a 9-hole muffin tin with medium-sized paper muffin cases (like cup-cake cases).

2 Put the cottage cheese into a bowl with all but 15 g (½ oz) of the Parmesan, the soya flour, ground almonds, baking powder, sun-blush tomatoes, basil, water and eggs and season with salt and pepper, then mix all together.

3 Spoon the mixture into the muffin cases, scatter with the remaining Parmesan and bake in a preheated oven, 200°C (400°F), Gas Mark 6, for 20 minutes, or until set, risen and golden brown. Serve as soon as possible – they're lovely eaten warm.

Honey corn muffins

MAKES 12
PREPARATION 20 MINUTES
COOKING 10–15 MINUTES

75 g (3 oz) wholemeal flour
100 g (3½ oz) coarse cornmeal
  or polenta
2½ teaspoons baking powder
30 g (1¼ oz) sunflower seeds
2 eggs
175 ml (6 fl oz) milk
6 tablespoons clear honey
2 tablespoons olive oil

1 Line a 12-hole muffin tin with 12 paper muffin cases.

2 Put the flour into a bowl with the cornmeal or polenta, the baking powder and half the sunflower seeds.

3 Whisk together the eggs, milk, honey and olive oil, then stir quickly into the dry ingredients – don't mix it too much.

4 Divide the mixture between the paper cases and sprinkle the remaining sunflower seeds on top of each muffin. Bake in a preheated oven, 200°C (400°F), Gas Mark 6, for 10–15 minutes until risen, golden and firm to a light touch. These muffins are delicious for breakfast straight from the oven, or can be reheated for a few minutes before serving.

Fruit fajita pudding

This sweet version of fajitas makes a fun help-yourself pudding, ideal for an informal meal with friends.

SERVES 4
PREPARATION 25 MINUTES
COOKING 15 MINUTES

FOR THE FAJITAS

125 g (4 oz) plain white flour
2 teaspoons caster sugar
2 eggs
300 ml (½ pint) milk and water mixed
a little flavourless oil, such as
   groundnut, for shallow-frying

FOR THE FRUIT SALAD

2 ripe pears, peeled and cut into
   bite-sized pieces
125 g (4 oz) small strawberries, hulled
125 g (4 oz) purple or red seedless
   grapes, halved
2 ripe kiwi fruit, peeled and sliced
juice of 1 orange

TO SERVE

toasted almonds or coconut
whipped double cream
real maple syrup
caster sugar
slices of lime

1 All the preparation for this can be done in advance. First make the fajitas, which are in fact sweet pancakes. Put the flour, sugar, eggs and most of the milk and water into a blender or food processor and blend to a smooth batter, adding the rest of the liquid if necessary to make a consistency like single cream. Alternatively, sift the flour into a bowl, add the sugar and break in the eggs. Beat together, adding the liquid gradually to make a smooth batter.

2 Heat 1 tablespoon of oil in a frying pan. When it's hot, swirl the oil around the pan and tip any excess into a cup. Pour in a good 2 tablespoons of the batter and tip the pan so that it spreads all over the base – you may need a bit more or less batter, depending on the size of your frying pan, but the pancakes need to be thick enough to be rolled around the fruit salad filling later – more robust than delicate crêpes!

3 After a minute or so, when the top of the pancake has set, flip it over with a palette knife and cook the other side, which will take only a few seconds. Put the pancake on to a plate and continue to make more in the same way, piling them up on the plate. Grease the frying pan with more oil as required.

4 Make the fruit salad by mixing all the fruits together and adding the orange juice. Put into a serving bowl and keep cool.

5 Serve a pile of fajitas with the bowl of fruit salad and small bowls of toasted almonds or coconut, whipped double cream, maple syrup, caster sugar and lime slices, for people to help themselves. Plenty of napkins and finger bowls might be a good idea.

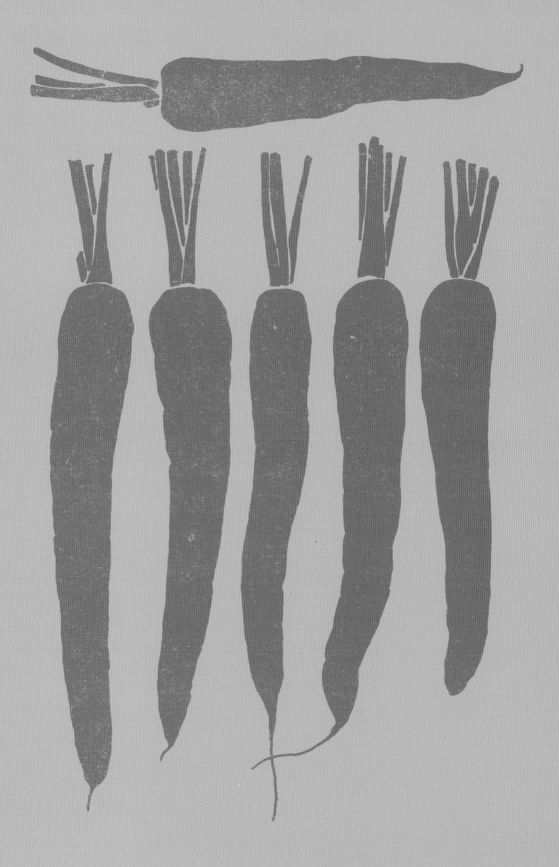

Parties & celebrations

Canapés: bruschette with three toppings

MAKES 24
PREPARATION 40 MINUTES
COOKING 30 MINUTES

1 baguette
olive oil
dried rosemary
salt and pepper

FOR THE AUBERGINE CAVIAR

2 aubergines, stems trimmed
1–2 garlic cloves, crushed
2 tablespoons tahini
2 tablespoons olive oil
2 tablespoons lemon juice
garlic sprouts, to garnish (optional)

FOR THE GOATS' CHEESE WITH RED
ONION AND BEETROOT

1 tablespoon olive oil
450 g (14½ oz) red onions, thinly sliced
1 tablespoon caster sugar
1 tablespoon red wine vinegar
450 g (14½ oz) cooked beetroot, diced
200 g (7 oz) soft goats' cheese
rosemary leaves, to garnish

FOR THE CHESTNUT PÂTÉ

200 g (7 oz) vacuum pack whole
    peeled chestnuts
15 g (½ oz) butter
1 garlic clove, crushed
2 tablespoons lemon juice
finely chopped sweet red peppers from
    a jar and thyme sprigs, to garnish

1 Start by making the bruschette. Slice the bread, then brush each slice
   on both sides with olive oil and sprinkle each piece on both sides with
   a good pinch of crushed rosemary. Place the bread on a baking sheet
   and bake in a preheated oven, 150°C (300°F), Gas Mark 2, for about
   20 minutes, until crisp. Cool on wire racks. They can be made up to
   1 week in advance and kept in an airtight container.

2 Next, make the toppings. For the aubergine caviar, prick the aubergines
   in several places, then cook them under a preheated very hot grill for
   25–30 minutes, until soft and well charred. Cool slightly, then peel off
   the skin and put the aubergine into a food processor with the garlic,
   tahini, the 2 tablespoons olive oil and the lemon juice and whiz to a pale
   cream. Season with salt and pepper and chill until required.

3 For the caramelized onion and beetroot, heat the olive oil in a large
   saucepan, add the onions, cover and cook for about 15 minutes, until
   they're very tender, stirring them every 5 minutes. Add the sugar, wine
   vinegar and beetroot, then simmer gently, uncovered, for 10–15 minutes.
   Remove from the heat, season and cool.

4 For the chestnut pâté, put the chestnuts into a food processor with the
   butter, garlic and lemon juice. Whiz to a fairly smooth purée and season
   with salt and pepper.

5 To complete the bruschette, spread one-third of the bases with aubergine
   caviar and garnish with a drizzle of olive oil and a few garlic sprouts,
   if liked. Spread another third of the bases with goats' cheese, top with the
   caramelized onion and beetroot and a piece of rosemary. Spread the
   remaining bruschette with chestnut pâté and garnish with a dusting
   of paprika pepper or sweet red peppers and thyme sprigs.

Mini carrot & cardamom tarte tatins

With their crisp flaky pastry bases and glossy orange tops of tender, melting carrot, these are gorgeous and not difficult to make.

MAKES 16
PREPARATION 25 MINUTES, PLUS
   COOLING
COOKING 35 MINUTES

750 g (1½ lb) carrots,
   very thinly sliced
1 large garlic clove, crushed
3 tablespoons olive oil
175 ml (6 fl oz) water
1½ teaspoons caster sugar
20 cardamom pods
375 g (12 oz) frozen ready-rolled
   all-butter puff pastry (see page 295)
salt and pepper

1 Put the carrots into a saucepan with the garlic, olive oil, water, sugar and some salt and pepper.

2 Crush the cardamom and discard the pods. Crush the seeds a little, then add to the saucepan. Bring to the boil, then reduce the heat, cover and cook gently for about 10 minutes, or until the carrots are tender and glossy, and the water has disappeared. If there is still water left, remove the lid of the pan and boil the liquid rapidly until it has disappeared. Cool.

3 Line a 22 x 32 cm (8½ x 12½ inch) Swiss roll tin with nonstick baking paper. Spread the carrots evenly over the bottom and cover with the pastry, pressing it down and trimming it to fit. Prick the pastry all over, then bake in a preheated oven, 200°C (400°F), Gas Mark 6, for 15 minutes until puffy, golden brown and crisp.

4 Leave the tart to cool completely, then turn it out on to a board so that the carrot is on top. Using a 3.5 cm (1½ inches) plain round cutter, carefully cut out 16 circles. You may need to use a sharp knife in addition to the cutter to get through the pastry.

5 Just before serving, put the little tarte tatins on to an ovenproof serving dish and pop them into the oven for a few minutes to warm through.

Mini watercress roulade slices

These are really very easy to do, and look and taste impressive.

MAKES 18
PREPARATION 25 MINUTES
COOKING 15 MINUTES

25 g (1 oz) butter
150 g (5 oz) packets watercress,
   finely chopped
3 eggs
150 g (5 oz) garlic and herb
   cream cheese
salt and pepper

1 Melt the butter in a saucepan, add the watercress and cook over a moderate heat for about 3 minutes, or until the watercress has wilted.

2 Purée the watercress in a food processor, then add the eggs and some salt and pepper and whiz until combined.

3 Line a 22 x 32 cm (8½ x 12½ inch) Swiss roll tin with nonstick baking paper. Pour the mixture into the tin, making sure it flows into the corners. Bake in a preheated oven, 200°C (400°F), Gas Mark 6, for about 12 minutes, or until set. Remove from the oven and leave to cool.

4 Turn out the roulade out on to a piece of nonstick baking paper and strip off the backing paper.

5 Beat the cream cheese in a bowl until soft, adding 1–2 tablespoons of hot water if necessary, then spread evenly over the top of the roulade.

6 With the long side facing you, make an incision about 5 mm (¼ inch) in from the edge, but don't cut right through. Bend this piece of roulade up, pressing it against the filling, then continue to roll it firmly to make a small Swiss roll. Wrap in nonstick baking paper until required, then unwrap and cut into 18 little slices to serve.

Oriental omelette wraps

MAKES 20
PREPARATION 30 MINUTES
COOKING 15 MINUTES

10 cm (4 inch) piece of cucumber,
    peeled
4 spring onions
1 tablespoon rice vinegar
1 tablespoon shoyu or tamari
1 tablespoon mirin
4 eggs
toasted sesame oil, for frying
salt and pepper

TO GARNISH

sesame seeds
radish roses
spring onion tassels

1 Cut the cucumber and spring onions into matchsticks about 5 cm (2 inches) long. Put them into a shallow dish and add the rice vinegar, shoyu or tamari and the mirin, then mix gently and set aside.

2 Beat the eggs with some salt and pepper. Coat a frying pan thinly with sesame oil and heat.

3 Pour about 1 tablespoon of the beaten egg into the frying pan. Let it run a little, but tilt the frying pan so that the omelette stays as round as possible. When the top has set completely, lift the omelette from the pan with a fish slice, roll it up lightly, put it on a plate and continue making another 19 omelettes in the same way, until all the egg has been used.

4 Unroll one of the omelettes, put a few matchsticks of cucumber and one of spring onion in the centre and reroll it. Place on a serving dish, seam-side down. Make the rest in the same way, arranging them all around the edge of a plate, like the spokes of a wheel.

5 Sprinkle the omelettes with a few sesame seeds and put some radish roses and spring onion tassels in the centre of the plate to garnish. Keep cool until required.

Tiny tortillas

These are delectable as they are, garnished with a spoonful of chive soured cream, or served with a bowl of soured cream and chives for dipping.

MAKES 20
PREPARATION 15 MINUTES
COOKING 30 MINUTES

500 g (1 lb) potatoes, peeled and cut
 into even-sized pieces
4 spring onions, chopped
1 red pepper, cored, deseeded and
 very finely chopped
2 eggs, beaten
olive oil, for shallow-frying
50 g (2 oz) vegetarian Gruyère
 cheese or similar cheeses such as
 Emmenthal or Gouda, grated
5–6 cherry tomatoes, sliced
salt and pepper
150 ml (¼ pint) soured cream and
 2 tablespoons chopped chives, to
 garnish (optional)

1 Put the potatoes into a saucepan, cover with boiling water and cook for about 10 minutes, until they are just tender. Drain and cool.

2 Cut the potatoes into small cubes – about 2.5 cm (1 inch) – then mix with the spring onions, red pepper, eggs and some salt and pepper.

3 Heat a little olive oil in a frying pan. Put heaped dessertspoons of the tortilla mixture into the hot oil, forming them into circles, and cook gently for about 5 minutes, or until the bases of the tortillas are golden brown and the tops have more or less set. Drain on a plate lined with kitchen paper and keep cool until you want to serve them.

4 Place the tortillas, in a single layer, on a flat ovenproof plate. Top each tortilla with a little Gruyère and a slice of tomato, then pop them under a preheated hot grill or into a hot oven for about 5 minutes, or until they are heated through and the tops are golden brown. Garnish each with a teaspoon of soured cream and some chopped chives, if liked, and serve at once.

Mini feta & sun-dried tomato muffins

MAKES 30
PREPARATION 10 MINUTES
COOKING 10 MINUTES

2 tablespoons olive oil, plus extra
   for greasing
1 egg
2 tablespoons sun-dried tomato paste
2 tablespoons water
125 g (4 oz) plain white flour
2 teaspoons baking powder
200 g (7 oz) feta cheese, cut into
   tiny dice
8 sun-dried tomatoes in oil, drained
   and finely chopped
4 tablespoons lightly chopped basil
salt and pepper

1 Line the bases of a 12-hole mini-muffin tin, each hole measuring 1.5 cm (¾ inch) across and about 1.5 cm (¾ inch) deep, with circles of nonstick baking paper, then brush them with olive oil. Alternatively, line the tin with mini paper cases if you have them.

2 Beat together 2 tablespoons olive oil, the egg, tomato paste and water.

3 Sift together the flour and baking powder into a bowl, then mix in the feta, sun-dried tomatoes, basil and some salt and pepper. Make a well in the centre and add the egg mixture. Stir until just combined – do not over-mix.

4 Spoon into the prepared mini-muffin tin holes or cases, filling them well, and bake in a preheated oven, 190°C (375°F), Gas Mark 5, for about 8 minutes, or until golden brown.

5 Remove from the oven and leave for 5 minutes to settle, then slip them out of the tin with a knife and leave to cool on a wire rack.

6 The muffins can be reheated before serving: put them on an ovenproof plate and pop them into a preheated oven, 180°C (350°F), Gas Mark 4, for about 5 minutes, to heat through and puff up.

Pecorino bites

MAKES 12
PREPARATION 20 MINUTES
COOKING 20 MINUTES

450 g (14½ oz) potatoes, peeled
  and cut into even-sized pieces
2 tablespoons truffle oil
25 g (1 oz) vegetarian Pecorino cheese
  or Parmesan-style cheese, grated
1–2 teaspoons porcini mushrooms in a
  vegetarian white truffle paste (see
  page 295)
1 large egg, beaten
4–6 tablespoons dried breadcrumbs
rapeseed or groundnut oil, for
  deep-frying
salt and pepper

1 Put the potatoes into a saucepan, cover with boiling water and cook for about 15 minutes, or until tender. Drain thoroughly. Mash the potatoes with the truffle oil, Pecorino and some salt and pepper. Leave until cool enough to handle.

2 Divide the mixture into 12 equal portions. Flatten each piece, then put a small spoonful – about ⅛ teaspoon – of truffle paste on to the centre of each. Take each of the rounds, draw the sides up so that the truffle paste is enclosed, and form into a ball shape. Dip the balls first in beaten egg and then in dried breadcrumbs, so that they are completely coated.

3 Heat the rapeseed or groundnut oil in a wok to 180–190°C (350–375°F), or until a cube of bread browns in 30 seconds. Add the potato balls and deep-fry for 2–3 minutes, or until golden and crisp. Drain on kitchen paper. Serve hot, warm or cold.

Artichoke & green olive 'cake' with sizzling pine nuts & saffron cream

You can buy marinated artichoke hearts from a deli, use frozen bases or, for perfection, boil the bases of globe artichokes until tender, having first cut off all the leaves and removed the 'chokes'.

SERVES 6
PREPARATION 30 MINUTES
COOKING 1¼ HOURS

25 g (1 oz) butter, plus extra
   for greasing
1 tablespoon olive oil
500 g (1 lb) new potatoes, cut into
   2.5 mm (⅛ inch) slices
150 ml (¼ pint) water
500 g (1 lb) cooked artichoke bases or
   marinated hearts, roughly chopped
150 g (5 oz) large green olives, pitted
   and roughly chopped
4 tablespoons chopped parsley
50 g (2 oz) soft white breadcrumbs
4 eggs, beaten
150 ml (¼ pint) single cream
salt and pepper
flat leaf parsley, to garnish

FOR THE SAFFRON CREAM

300 ml (½ pint) double cream
½ teaspoon saffron threads

FOR THE TOPPING

25 g (1 oz) butter
1 tablespoon olive oil
4 garlic cloves, sliced
2 tablespoons pine nuts

1 Line a 1 kg (2 lb) loaf tin with a strip of nonstick baking paper and grease with butter.

2 Heat the butter and olive oil in a saucepan, then add the potatoes and water. Bring to the boil, then reduce the heat, cover and cook gently for 10–15 minutes, or until the potatoes are tender and most of the water has disappeared.

3 Mix together the potatoes and their cooking liquid, the artichokes, olives, parsley, breadcrumbs, eggs, single cream and salt and pepper to taste. Spoon the mixture into the prepared loaf tin and level the surface. Bake in a preheated oven, 180°C (350°F), Gas Mark 4, for 1 hour, or until it is firm and a skewer inserted into the centre comes out clean.

4 To make the saffron cream, put the double cream and saffron into a saucepan, bring to the boil, then season with salt and pepper. Leave to infuse until ready to serve, then reheat.

5 Turn out the 'cake' on to a warmed serving platter and keep warm while you make the pine nut topping. Heat the butter and olive oil in a saucepan and add the garlic and pine nuts. Cook over a moderate heat for a minute or two until the pine nuts and garlic are golden brown, then remove from the heat and pour, sizzling, over the top of the cake. Garnish with some flat leaf parsley and serve at once, with the saffron cream.

Baby Yorkshire puddings with nut roast & horseradish

These are fabulous, and not nearly as much work as you might think because they can be prepared in advance and then just reheated before serving – they'll puff up beautifully.

MAKES 24
PREPARATION 20 MINUTES,
 PLUS STANDING
COOKING 35 MINUTES

50 g (2 oz) plain white flour
1 egg
75 ml (3 fl oz) milk
75 ml (3 fl oz) water
2 tablespoons olive oil, plus extra
 for greasing
salt and pepper
horseradish sauce, to serve

FOR THE NUT ROAST

50 g (2 oz) almonds
25 g (1 oz) wholemeal bread
50 g (2 oz) grated cheese
50 g (2 oz) onion, roughly chopped
½ teaspoon dried mixed herbs
1 tablespoon shoyu or tamari

1 Sift the flour into a bowl with a pinch of salt. Make a well in the centre, break the egg into it and mix to a paste, then gradually draw in the flour. Mix the milk with the water, then stir into the bowl, but don't over-beat. Transfer the batter to a jug, so that it will be easy to pour into the tin, and leave to rest for 30 minutes. This allows the starch to swell, giving a lighter result.

2 Meanwhile, make the nut roast. Put all the ingredients into a food processor and whiz until you have a smooth mixture that holds together. Form it into 24 cocktail sausages, coat all over with olive oil and place on a baking sheet.

3 Use 2 x 12-hole nonstick mini-muffin tins, each hole measuring 1.5 cm (¾ inch) across and about 1.5 cm (¾ inch) deep. Put ½ teaspoon olive oil into each hole and put the tins into a preheated oven, 220°C (425°F), Gas Mark 7. The oil needs to heat for 10 minutes before you put the batter in.

4 Put the nut roast sausages in the oven at this point (they will take longer to cook than the Yorkshire puddings) and roast for about 15 minutes, or until they are brown and crisp.

5 When the oil in the muffin tins is smoking hot, quickly pour the batter into each hole, filling them about two-thirds full. Bake for 10 minutes, until puffed up and golden. Pop them out of the tin and cool on a wire rack.

6 When you want to serve the Yorkshire puddings, put them on a heatproof serving dish and place a small piece of nut roast on top of each. Put them in the oven, 220°C (425°F), Gas Mark 7, for 4–5 minutes, until hot and puffy. Serve immediately with horseradish sauce.

Little broad bean & mint risottos

Creamy risotto, served piping hot in little ramekins with tiny spoons, makes a sensational party dish and is very easy to do.

SERVES 24
PREPARATION 30 MINUTES
COOKING 30 MINUTES

300 g (10 oz) frozen broad beans
1 litre (1¾ pints) vegetable stock
1 tablespoon olive oil
bunch of spring onions, finely chopped
2 garlic cloves, finely chopped
400 g (13 oz) risotto rice
3–4 large mint sprigs
100 ml (3½ fl oz) dry white wine
50 g (2 oz) butter
100 g (3½ oz) Parmesan-style cheese,
    grated
salt and pepper
chopped mint, to garnish

1 Cook the broad beans in a saucepan of boiling water for 4–5 minutes, then drain and cool. Pop the bright green beans out of their grey skins and put to one side. Discard the skins.

2 To make the risotto, put the stock into a saucepan and bring to the boil, then reduce the heat and keep hot over a very gentle heat.

3 Heat the olive oil in a large saucepan, add the spring onions and stir, then cover and cook gently for 3–4 minutes, until tender but not browned. Stir in the garlic and cook for a minute or two longer.

4 Add the rice to the pan, along with the mint sprigs, and stir over a gentle heat for 2–3 minutes, or until the rice looks translucent, then pour in the wine and stir all the time as it bubbles away.

5 When the wine has disappeared, add a ladleful of the hot stock and stir over a low-to-medium heat until the rice has absorbed the stock. Add another ladleful and continue in this way, adding the broad beans with the final ladleful of stock, until you've used up all the stock, the rice is tender and the consistency creamy – about 15–20 minutes.

6 Remove the sprigs of mint, add the butter and half the Parmesan and season with salt and pepper. Immediately transfer the risotto into warmed ramekins, scatter each with a little Parmesan and chopped mint and serve at once, each with a tiny spoon.

Wild mushroom roulade

SERVES 6
PREPARATION 20 MINUTES
COOKING 25 MINUTES

20 g (¾ oz) flat leaf parsley, chopped
175 g (6 oz) low-fat soft cream cheese
175 g (6 oz) vegetarian Gruyère
    cheese or similar cheeses such as
    Emmenthal or Gouda, finely grated
4 eggs, separated
salt and pepper
Tomato sauce (see page 117), to serve

FOR THE FILLING

1 tablespoon olive oil
500 g (1 lb) mixed wild mushrooms
    or oyster mushrooms, wiped
4 garlic cloves, finely chopped
150 g (5 oz) garlic and herb
    cream cheese
1–2 tablespoons hot water

1 Line a 23 x 33 cm (9 x 13 inch) Swiss roll tin with nonstick baking paper so that it extends about 5 cm (2 inches) on all sides.

2 Set aside half the parsley for the garnish. Put into a large bowl with the low-fat cheese, the Gruyère and the egg yolks. Mix well and season with salt and pepper.

3 In another bowl, whisk the egg whites until they stand in stiff peaks, then, using a large metal spoon, fold them lightly into the Gruyère mixture.

4 Pour the mixture into the prepared Swiss roll tin, spreading it evenly into the corners. Bake in a preheated oven, 200°C (400°F), Gas Mark 6, for 12 minutes, or until firm, golden brown and well risen.

5 While the roulade is cooking, make the filling. Heat the olive oil in a large saucepan, add the mushrooms and garlic and fry over quite a high heat until the mushrooms are tender – 4–5 minutes. You can assemble the roulade at this point, or you can do it after the roulade has cooled when it can be a little easier to roll.

6 Put a large piece of nonstick baking paper, a little bigger than the roulade, on the work surface and turn out the cooked roulade on to it. Strip off the backing paper.

7 Mix the garlic and herb cream cheese with enough hot water to soften it a little, then spread it evenly over the roulade. Arrange the mushrooms on top, taking them to within 1 cm (½ inch) of the short edges. Make sure any thick mushroom stems are parallel with the short edges – this makes it easier to roll them up. Now for the fun! Starting with one short end, fold up about 1 cm (½ inch) of the roulade and press it down firmly. Using the paper to help you and holding the folded end through the paper, start rolling firmly, then press the roulade into a good shape when it's rolled up.

8 Put the roulade, seam-side down, on to a heatproof serving plate. Now either reheat it in the oven for 5–10 minutes until piping hot, or let it go cold and reheat it later for 10–15 minutes. It will puff up a bit and smell divine.

9 Garnish the top with the reserved parsley and cut into thick slices to serve, with the tomato sauce.

Christmas galette

This galette is full of Christmas flavours. Serve it with roast potatoes and cranberry sauce.

SERVES 6
PREPARATION 30 MINUTES,
    PLUS CHILLING
COOKING 30–35 MINUTES

375 g (12 oz) fine wholemeal flour
    or half wholemeal, half white
175 g (6 oz) butter, cut into
    rough chunks
½ teaspoon salt
3 tablespoons cold water
2 tablespoons olive oil

FOR THE FILLING

375 g (12 oz) carrots, scraped and
    cut into rings
375 g (12 oz) leeks, trimmed and
    cut into 2.5cm (1 inch) pieces
275 g (9 oz) shallots
375 g (12 oz) trimmed baby
    Brussels sprouts
2 Cox apples, peeled, cored
    and chopped
100 g (3½ oz) cashew nuts
salt and pepper
chopped parsley, to garnish

FOR THE SAUCE

50 g (2 oz) butter
2 tablespoons cornflour or arrowroot
200 ml (7 fl oz) soya milk
175 g (6 oz) Stilton cheese, crumbled

1 To make the pastry, put the flour, butter and salt into a food processor and whiz until it resembles coarse breadcrumbs. Alternatively, put the ingredients into a bowl and rub the butter into the flour with your fingertips. Add the water and mix to a dough.

2 Turn out the dough on to a lightly floured surface. Knead briefly, then form into a circle and roll out to fit a round flan tin measuring 30 cm (12 inches) across and 3.5cm (1½ inches) deep. Trim the edges, prick the base thoroughly all over, then chill for 30 minutes.

3 Bake the tart in a preheated oven, 200°C (400°F), Gas Mark 6, for 20 minutes, until the pastry is 'set' and lightly browned. A minute or two before you take it out of the oven, heat the olive oil in a small saucepan until smoking hot. As soon as the tart comes out of the oven, pour the hot olive oil all over the base – it will sizzle and almost 'fry'. This will 'waterproof' the base of the tart so that it will remain crisp.

4 Meanwhile, to make the filling, half-fill a large saucepan with water and bring to the boil. Add the carrots, leeks and shallots, bring back to the boil, cover and cook for 5 minutes, then add the sprouts, cover and cook for a further 6–7 minutes, until all the vegetables are tender. Drain.

5 To make the sauce, melt the butter in a saucepan and stir in the cornflour or arrowroot. When it froths at the edges, pour in the soya milk and stir over the heat until it has thickened. Remove from the heat and stir in the Stilton. Season with salt and pepper.

6 Mix the sauce with the drained vegetables and the apple. Check the seasoning, then spoon into the tart case and top with the cashews. Put back into the oven for 10–15 minutes, until the filling is piping hot and the cashews are golden brown. Scatter with chopped parsley and serve at once.

Moroccan-flavoured aubergine Wellington ⓥ

SERVES 6
PREPARATION 20 MINUTES, PLUS
   COOLING
COOKING 1 HOUR

125 g (4 oz) couscous
2 tablespoons olive oil
1 onion, chopped
1 aubergine, cut into 1 cm (½ inch)
   cubes
1 red pepper, cored, deseeded and cut
   into 1 cm (½ inch) pieces
25 g (1 oz) ready-to-eat dried apricots,
   chopped
25 g (1 oz) raisins
2 garlic cloves, crushed
1 tablespoon ground cinnamon
1 tablespoon ground cumin
1 tablespoon chopped mint
1 tablespoon chopped parsley
100 g (3½ oz) toasted flaked almonds
125 g (4 oz) pitted black olives, sliced
2 x 350 g (11½ oz) sheets of
   ready-rolled puff pastry
soya milk, for brushing
sesame seeds, for sprinkling
salt and pepper

1 Put the couscous into a bowl, cover with boiling water and leave to soak.

2 Meanwhile, heat the olive oil in a large saucepan, add the onion and fry for 5 minutes, then add the aubergine and red pepper, cover and cook gently for 10–15 minutes, or until the vegetables are tender. Add the apricots, raisins, garlic, cinnamon and cumin and stir over the heat for a minute or two until the spices smell aromatic. Remove from the heat.

3 Drain the couscous thoroughly in a sieve and add it to the pan, along with the mint, parsley, almonds and olives. Season with salt and pepper to taste and leave the mixture to cool.

4 Spread a pastry sheet out on a baking sheet and brush with soya milk.

5 Put the aubergine mixture in the centre of the pastry. Place the second sheet of pastry over the top and press the edges together. Trim the edges, leaving a 2.5 cm (1 inch) border. Pinch the edges with your fingers and thumbs. Brush with soya milk and sprinkle with sesame seeds.

6 Bake in a preheated oven, 200°C (400°F), Gas Mark 6, for 40 minutes, until the pastry has puffed up and is golden brown. Transfer to a warmed serving platter and serve at once.

Luscious vegan pumpkin pie ⓥ

SERVES 6
PREPARATION 30 MINUTES,
   PLUS PUMPKIN BAKING
COOKING 40 MINUTES

300 g (10 oz) fine wholemeal flour
   or half wholemeal, half white
150 g (5 oz) vegan margarine or
   butter, cut into rough chunks
½ teaspoon salt
2–3 tablespoons cold water
2–3 tablespoons soya milk
caster sugar, for dredging
ground cinnamon, for sprinkling
thick cream or yogurt, to serve

FOR THE FILLING

500 g (1 lb) canned pumpkin purée or
   1 kg (2lb) pumpkin
275 g (9 oz) firm tofu, drained, patted
   dry and broken into chunks
125 g (4 oz) soft brown sugar
1 tablespoon black treacle
1 teaspoon ground cinnamon
½ teaspoon ground ginger
½ teaspoon grated nutmeg

1   If you are using fresh pumpkin, small ones (or butternut squash) are best. Halve, deseed and place, cut-side down, on a baking sheet. Bake in a preheated oven, 200°C (400°F), Gas Mark 6, until tender – 40–60 minutes, depending on the size of the pumpkin.

2   Meanwhile, make the pastry. Put the flour, vegan margarine or butter and salt into a food processor and whiz until it resembles coarse breadcrumbs. Alternatively, put the ingredients into a bowl and rub the fat into the flour with your fingertips. Add the water and mix to a dough.

3   Turn out the dough on to a lightly floured surface. Knead briefly, then form into a circle and roll out to fit a 23 cm (9 inch) round flan dish. Trim the edges and reserve the trimmings.

4   To make the filling, remove the pumpkin skin if using fresh pumpkin and chop the flesh. Put the pumpkin into a food processor with the tofu, soft brown sugar, treacle and spices and whiz to a thick, smooth purée. Pour into the flan case and gently smooth the surface.

5   Reroll the pastry trimmings, brush with soya milk, dredge with a little caster sugar and sprinkle with cinnamon. Cut into strips and arrange in a lattice on top of the pumpkin filling. As well as looking attractive, this topping will become crisp, contrasting with the soft filling and helping to hold it together.

6   Bake the pie in a preheated oven, 180°C (350°F), Gas Mark 4, for 40 minutes, until the filling is just set and the topping crisp. Serve hot, warm or cold, with vegan ice cream or cream or, for vegetarians, thick cream or yogurt.

Dreamy raspberry & rose pavlova

This pavlova looks sensational yet is easy to make. You can even make it in advance and freeze it in a rigid container. To use, put on a serving dish and allow 1–2 hours to defrost before decorating.

SERVES 6
PREPARATION 20 MINUTES
COOKING 1¼ HOURS

4 egg whites
250 g (8 oz) caster sugar
2 teaspoons cornflour
1 teaspoon red or white wine vinegar
1 teaspoon vanilla extract
300 ml (½ pint) double cream
2 teaspoons triple-distilled rosewater
375 g (12 oz) raspberries
a few red or pink rose petals, to decorate

1 Line a large baking sheet with nonstick baking paper.

2 Put the egg whites into a large, clean, grease-free bowl and whisk until they are thick, glossy and standing in peaks.

3 Mix together the sugar and cornflour, then add to the egg whites in 2 or 3 batches, whisking all the time to achieve a beautiful, glossy white meringue mixture. Finally, stir in the wine vinegar and vanilla extract.

4 Spoon the mixture on to the baking paper, gently spreading it out into a circle 20–23 cm (8–9 inches) in diameter. Place in a preheated oven, 180°C (350°F), Gas Mark 4, turn the heat down to 150°C (300°F), Gas Mark 2, and bake for 1¼ hours, or until crisp. Leave to cool in the oven if possible.

5 To finish the pavlova, whip the cream until it forms soft peaks, then whisk in the rosewater. Heap this on top of the pavlova, cover with the raspberries and shower with rose petals. Serve as soon as possible, though it's still easy to eat even after 24 hours.

Jam & cream sponges

These are like darling little Victoria sponge cakes! The discarded 'cuttings' of cake, jam and cream make a great base for a quick trifle, with some fruit, custard and jelly.

MAKES 20
PREPARATION 20 MINUTES, PLUS
   COOLING
COOKING 15–20 MINUTES

125 g (4 oz) butter, softened
125 g (4 oz) caster sugar
2 eggs
125 g (4 oz) self-raising flour
1 teaspoon baking powder
1 tablespoon water
icing sugar, for dusting

FOR THE FILLING

3–4 tablespoons raspberry jam
150 ml (¼ pint) double cream,
   whipped

1 Whisk together the butter, sugar, eggs, flour, baking powder and water until light and creamy.

2 Line a 22 x 32 cm (8½ x 12½ inch) Swiss roll tin with nonstick baking paper. Spoon the mixture into the tin, spreading it to the edges and into the corners. Bake in a preheated oven, 160°C (325°F), Gas Mark 3, for 15–20 minutes, until risen and firm to a light touch. Remove from the tin and leave to cool on a wire rack.

3 When the cake is completely cold, lay it face down on a board and carefully strip off the backing paper. Cut the cake into 2 equal halves and spread one of them with first the jam and then the cream. Press the other half on top, gently but firmly. Using a 3.5 cm (1½ inch) plain round cutter, cut out 20 circles, then put them on to a plate. (They may look neatest upside down – that way if the sponge on top cracks a bit as you cut it, it won't show.)

4 When the cakes are all done, dust with icing sugar and keep them in a cool place until required.

Berry skewers with white chocolate dip

MAKES 20
PREPARATION 15 MINUTES
COOKING 5 MINUTES

200 g (7 oz) mixed berries, such as
strawberries (halved), large
blueberries, raspberries, blackberries
or baby kiwis (halved)

FOR THE WHITE CHOCOLATE DIP

100 g (3½ oz) white chocolate,
broken into pieces
125 ml (4 fl oz) double cream

1 To make the dip, melt the chocolate in a heatproof bowl set over a pan
of gently steaming water. Remove from the heat and stir in the cream.
Put into a small serving bowl and leave to cool.

2 Put one or two berries on each small skewer or cocktail stick – enough
for a mouthful. Arrange the skewers around the bowl of white chocolate
dip and serve.

Pecan & tarragon-stuffed apricots ⓥ

This is a delicious treat for your vegan party guests, though everyone will enjoy it. You can get vegan cream cheese at good healthfood shops and many large supermarkets.

MAKES ABOUT 26
PREPARATION 15 MINUTES,
   PLUS SOAKING

250 g (8 oz) ready-to-eat dried apricots
300 ml (½ pint) apple juice
225 g (7½ oz) vegan herb and garlic
   cream cheese
50 g (2 oz) pecan nuts
small bunch of tarragon

1 Put the apricots into a bowl, cover with the apple juice and leave to soak for 8 hours, or overnight.

2 Drain the apricots and blot with kitchen paper. Stuff each apricot with 1 teaspoon of the cream cheese, a small sprig of tarragon and a pecan nut. Arrange them, stuffing-side up, on a serving platter.

Side dishes

Sesame-roasted asparagus with wasabi vinaigrette ⓥ

If you can make the dressing in advance – 24 hours is not too long – the flavour of the wasabi mellows and is delicious and refreshing with the asparagus.

SERVES 4
PREPARATION 10 MINUTES
COOKING 15–20 MINUTES

500 g (1 lb) asparagus, trimmed
2 tablespoons toasted sesame oil
salt

FOR THE WASABI VINAIGRETTE

1 packet (2 teaspoons) wasabi powder
2 tablespoons warm water
1 tablespoon rice vinegar
1 tablespoon flavourless vegetable oil,
   such as grapeseed
2 tablespoons toasted sesame oil
salt and pepper

1 Toss the asparagus in the sesame oil, spread out on a baking sheet and sprinkle with salt. Roast in a preheated oven, 220°C (425°F), Gas Mark 7, for about 15 minutes, or until just tender and lightly browned in places.

2 To make the vinaigrette, put the wasabi into a lidded jar, add the warm water and mix to a paste. Add the rice vinegar, vegetable oil, sesame oil and some salt and pepper, put the lid on and shake vigorously for a few seconds until smooth.

3 Arrange the asparagus on individual plates and drizzle the vinaigrette on top. Serve hot, warm or cold.

Braised whole baby carrots & fennel ⓥ

These vegetables melt in your mouth and their golden liquid supplies a natural sauce for the dish. They are also very forgiving: they should be really tender, so it's almost impossible to overcook them, and they can be cooked in advance and gently reheated later if this is most convenient. If there are any left over, they also taste very good cold.

SERVES 4
PREPARATION 15 MINUTES
COOKING 30 MINUTES

2 bunches (about 750 g/1½ lb) of
  baby carrots
400 g (13 oz) baby fennel
4 tablespoons olive oil
4 garlic cloves, sliced
300 ml (½ pint) water
1 tablespoon lemon juice
salt and pepper
chopped parsley, to garnish

1 If the carrots are really young, just scrub them; if they're older, peel them, but in either case keep them whole and leave 1 cm (½ inch) or so of the green stems attached at the top. If the fennel is really young and tender, just trim the tops.

2 Put the carrots and fennel into a saucepan with the olive oil, garlic, water, lemon juice and some salt and pepper and bring to the boil. Reduce the heat, cover and cook gently for about 30 minutes, checking occasionally to make sure they're not sticking. They're done when they feel very tender to the point of a knife and the water has reduced to a syrupy golden glaze. Scatter with chopped parsley and serve.

Parsnips in sage butter

A simple yet wonderful combination of flavours.

SERVES 4
PREPARATION 10 MINUTES
COOKING 15–20 MINUTES

500 g (1 lb) baby parsnips
25 g (1 oz) butter, softened
1 tablespoon chopped sage
salt and pepper

1 Cut the parsnips lengthways into quarters, to give long slim pieces. Put them into a saucepan, cover with water and bring to the boil, then reduce the heat and simmer for 10–15 minutes, or until tender.

2 Blend the butter with the sage and set aside.

3 Drain the parsnips and put into a warm serving dish, or return them to the saucepan. Season with salt and pepper, then add the sage butter and serve.

Cabbage with sesame & ginger ⓥ

This very simple treatment transforms cabbage. It goes particularly well with Asian-style dishes.

SERVES 4

PREPARATION 5 MINUTES

COOKING 5 MINUTES

1 sweetheart or similar cabbage, shredded

1 tablespoon toasted sesame oil

1 tablespoon grated fresh root ginger

1 garlic clove, crushed

salt and pepper

1 Bring 2.5 cm (1 inch) depth of water to the boil in a saucepan, add the cabbage, bring back to the boil, cover and cook for about 5 minutes, or until the cabbage is tender. Drain.

2 Add the sesame oil, ginger and garlic to the cabbage and stir well. Season with salt and pepper and serve at once.

Roast potatoes in sea salt & balsamic vinegar ⓥ

Having tried various different oils for roasting potatoes, I've found that rapeseed or groundnut oil give the crispiest results.

SERVES 4
PREPARATION 15 MINUTES
COOKING 45 MINUTES

1 kg (2 lb) potatoes, peeled and
  cut into 1 cm (½ inch) chunks
rapeseed or groundnut oil, for roasting
salt and pepper
balsamic vinegar

1 Put the potatoes into a saucepan, cover with water and bring to the boil, then reduce the heat and simmer for 7 minutes.

2 Pour 5 mm (¼ inch) of oil into a roasting tin large enough to hold the potatoes in a single layer, then put into a preheated oven, 200°C (400°F), Gas Mark 6, until smoking hot.

3 Drain the potatoes and put them back into the saucepan, then put the lid on the pan and shake to roughen the outsides and make them cook more crisply.

4 Tip the potatoes into the hot oil and turn them with a large spoon so that the oil covers them all over. Roast for about 35 minutes, or until the potatoes are golden and crisp, turning them over when the undersides are done.

5 Using a slotted spoon, transfer the potatoes to a warm serving dish. Sprinkle generously with salt and pepper, drizzle with balsamic vinegar and serve.

Saffron & garlic mash

SERVES 4
PREPARATION 15 MINUTES,
   PLUS STEEPING
COOKING 20 MINUTES

1.1 kg (2¼ lb) potatoes, peeled and
   cut into even-sized pieces
150 ml (¼ pint) single cream
good pinch of saffron threads
50 g (2 oz) butter
4 garlic cloves, crushed
salt and pepper

FOR THE GARNISH

4 garlic cloves
1 tablespoon olive oil
1 tablespoon chopped parsley

1   Put the potatoes into a saucepan, cover with boiling water and cook for about 20 minutes, or until tender.

2   Meanwhile, put the cream into a small saucepan with the saffron and bring almost to the boil, then remove from the heat, cover and leave to steep.

3   To make the garnish, cut the garlic cloves into thin slices. Heat the olive oil in a small pan, add the garlic and fry for a minute or so until the garlic is golden. Remove from the heat and set aside.

4   Drain the potatoes, reserving the water, then mash with the butter, crushed garlic and saffron-infused cream (no need to remove the saffron threads) to make a smooth, creamy consistency. Add a small quantity of the reserved cooking water if needed. Season with salt and pepper.

5   Spoon the potato into a warmed serving dish, top with the fried pieces of garlic and the oil and some chopped parsley, and serve.

Butter bean & herb mash with pak choi v

SERVES 4
PREPARATION 15 MINUTES
COOKING 10 MINUTES

2 x 410 g (13½ oz) cans butter beans
2 garlic cloves
1–2 tablespoons lemon juice
4 spring onions, chopped
2 tablespoons chopped parsley
salt and pepper

FOR THE PAK CHOI

500 g (1 lb) pak choi or other Asian
    leaves, large pieces halved or
    quartered
1 tablespoon soy sauce
1 tablespoon lemon juice
1 tablespoon toasted sesame oil
1 tablespoon toasted sesame seeds

1 Drain the butter beans, reserving the liquid. Either mash the beans roughly using a fork or potato masher or, for a smoother mash, whiz them in a food processor.

2 Put the mashed beans into a saucepan with the garlic, lemon juice, spring onions, parsley and enough of the reserved bean liquid to make the consistency of mashed potatoes. Season with salt and pepper. Heat gently and keep warm.

3 Bring 2.5 cm (1 inch) depth of water to the boil in a large saucepan. Add the pak choi or other leaves, bring back to the boil, cover and cook for 2–6 minutes, or until it's just tender – the timing will depend on the exact type of leaves and the size of the pieces. Drain in a colander, then return to the pan.

4 Add the soy sauce, lemon juice, sesame oil and sesame seeds to the leaves and swirl around to coat them all. Serve with the butter bean mash.

Lentils with portobellos, garlic & red wine •

This is delicious with mashed potatoes or just lots of lightly cooked cabbage. If you prefer, you can use cooked Puy lentils instead of green lentils.

SERVES 4
PREPARATION 15 MINUTES
COOKING 45 MINUTES

1 tablespoon olive oil
2 onions, chopped
4 garlic cloves, finely chopped
8 portobello mushrooms
2 tomatoes, chopped
a few thyme sprigs
2 bay leaves
410 g (13½ oz) can green lentils
250 ml (8 fl oz) red wine
2 teaspoons Dijon mustard
salt and pepper
chopped parsley, to garnish

1 Heat the olive oil in a large saucepan, add the onions, cover and cook for 5 minutes. Add the garlic, mushrooms, tomatoes and herbs and stir until lightly coated with the oil. Cover the pan and cook gently for a further 10 minutes.

2 Add the lentils, together with their liquid, and the wine, bring to the boil, then cover and leave to simmer over a gentle heat for 30 minutes.

3 Put the mustard into a small bowl, add a little liquid from the pan and stir to make a smooth cream, then tip this into the pan and stir again. Season with salt and pepper. Garnish with the parsley and serve.

Spicy Thai noodles

SERVES 4
PREPARATION 15 MINUTES
COOKING 20 MINUTES

250 g (8 oz) rice noodles
2 tablespoons toasted sesame oil
2 teaspoons vegetarian Thai red
   curry paste
6 spring onions, finely sliced
walnut-sized piece of fresh root ginger,
   peeled and cut into thin shreds
2 garlic cloves, crushed
2–3 tablespoons rice vinegar
1–2 tablespoons shoyu or tamari
2 tablespoons chopped coriander
salt and pepper

1 Put the noodles into a bowl, cover with boiling water and leave to soak for 5 minutes, until tender, then drain and toss in 1 tablespoon of the sesame oil to prevent the noodles from sticking together. Alternatively, prepare according to the packet instructions.

2 Meanwhile, heat the rest of the sesame oil in a large saucepan, add the curry paste and let it sizzle for a few seconds. Add the spring onions, ginger and garlic and stir-fry for 1–2 minutes, to cook lightly.

3 Add the noodles to the pan and remove from the heat. Add the rice vinegar, shoyu or tamari and some salt and pepper and toss lightly. Stir in the chopped coriander and serve.

Tandoori paneer

You need a lot of ingredients for this really quick and simple recipe, and it's always popular! You can also make a very good vegan version by using firm tofu instead of paneer.

SERVES 4
PREPARATION 10 MINUTES
COOKING 10–15 MINUTES

2 x 225 g (7½ oz) blocks paneer,
    each cut into 1 cm (½ inch) cubes
salt
2 tablespoons roughly chopped
    coriander, to garnish
lemon wedges and naan bread, to serve

FOR THE SPICE MIXTURE

1 tablespoon grated fresh root ginger
1 tablespoon crushed garlic
½ teaspoon hot paprika or
    chilli powder
1 teaspoon turmeric
1 tablespoon ground cumin
2 tablespoons rapeseed oil
2 tablespoons lemon juice

FOR THE VEGETABLE GARNISH

4 tomatoes, sliced
1 small onion, sliced
1 green pepper, cored, deseeded
    and sliced

FOR THE MINT RAITA

300 g (10 oz) natural yogurt
    (dairy or vegan)
4 tablespoons chopped mint
salt and pepper

1 To make the raita, mix the yogurt with the mint and season with salt and pepper to taste. Put into a serving bowl and set aside.

2 To make the spice mixture, put all the ingredients into a bowl and mix together.

3 Toss the cubes of paneer in the spice mixture and stir to coat them, adding a little salt to taste, remembering that paneer is quite salty.

4 Spread the cubes of paneer out on a grill pan or on a baking sheet that will fit under your grill and cook under a preheated grill for 10–15 minutes, turning them a couple of times, until sizzling and crisp.

5 Meanwhile, to make the garnish, mix together the tomatoes, onion and green pepper and put into a serving bowl or on to individual plates. Serve the paneer straight from the grill, hot and sizzling, with the salad garnish, a scattering of coriander on top and lemon wedges. Eat with warm naan bread and some mint raita.

Leek rice with almonds & red pepper mayo ⓥ

SERVES 4
PREPARATION 20 MINUTES
COOKING 20–25 MINUTES

250 g (8 oz) white basmati rice
1 teaspoon turmeric
450 ml (¾ pint) water
450 g (14½ oz) leeks, cut into 2.5 cm
    (1 inch) pieces
2 tablespoons lemon juice
1 tablespoon olive oil
2 teaspoons black mustard seeds
4 tablespoons toasted flaked almonds
50 g (2 oz) small green olives, pitted
salt and pepper

FOR THE RED PEPPER MAYO

1 large red pepper, halved, cored
    and deseeded
2 tablespoons red wine vinegar
6 tablespoons olive oil
2 teaspoons caster sugar

1 Put the rice into a saucepan with the turmeric and water. Bring to
   the boil, then reduce the heat as low as possible, cover and leave to cook
   for about 10 minutes. Remove from the heat and leave to stand, still
   covered, for 5–10 minutes.

2 Meanwhile, cook the leeks in a saucepan of boiling water for about
   10 minutes, or until tender. Drain.

3 Add the lemon juice to the rice along with some salt and pepper,
   stirring gently, then mix the leeks into the rice.

4 Heat the olive oil in a small frying pan, add the mustard seeds and fry for
   1–2 minutes, or until they're sizzling. Add to the leek mixture, along
   with the almonds and olives.

5 Meanwhile, to make the mayo, put the red pepper halves cut-side down
   on a grill pan and cook under a preheated hot grill for about 10 minutes,
   or until black and blistered in places. Cool, then strip off the skin. Blend
   the peppers with the wine vinegar, olive oil, sugar and some salt and
   pepper in a food processor, blender or using a stick blender, to make a
   smooth, thick, brick-red sauce. Serve with the rice. This dish can be
   served hot, warm or cold.

Buckwheat & mango tabbouleh ⓥ

You can buy buckwheat at organic and healthfood shops. Be sure to get the raw, untoasted type.

SERVES 4
PREPARATION 10 MINUTES,
   PLUS STANDING
COOKING 3–4 MINUTES

250 g (8 oz) raw buckwheat
1 large ripe juicy mango
bunch of mint, chopped
juice of 1 lime
salt and pepper

1 Put the buckwheat into a dry saucepan and stir over a moderate heat for 3–4 minutes, or until the buckwheat smells toasty and is turning light golden brown. Remove from the heat, cover with boiling water and leave to stand for 10–15 minutes, until softened.

2 Meanwhile, make two cuts through the mango straight down about 5 mm (¼ inch) either side of the stalk, to cut the flesh from the flat stone. Peel off the skin and cut the flesh into rough pieces; remove as much flesh from around the stone as you can. Put all the mango flesh into a bowl.

3 When the buckwheat has softened – when you can squash a grain between your finger and thumb – drain it and put into a bowl. Stir in the mango, mint, lime juice and some salt and pepper. Eat at once or store in a cool place for a few hours.

Jamaican jerk sweet potato

It's easy to make your own jerk paste, but for a very fast option, use a shop-bought one instead.

SERVES 4
PREPARATION 20 MINUTES
COOKING 10 MINUTES

4 sweet potatoes, about 350 g
   (11½ oz) each
lime wedges and soft bread, to serve
   (optional)

FOR THE JERK SPICE PASTE

1 onion, roughly chopped
1 red chilli, deseeded
4 garlic cloves
4 teaspoons dried thyme
2 teaspoons allspice
1 teaspoon ground cinnamon
½ teaspoon ground nutmeg
2 tablespoons olive oil
1 teaspoon salt
1 teaspoon pepper

FOR THE CHIVE YOGURT

2 tablespoons chopped chives
300 g (10 oz) natural yogurt
salt and pepper

1 To make the jerk paste, put all the ingredients into a food processor and whiz to a paste.

2 Cut the sweet potatoes into wedges about 5 mm (¼ inch) thick – they need to be thin enough to cook through without burning. Spread the cut surfaces of the wedges with the jerk paste and cook under a preheated hot grill or on a barbecue for 5 minutes on each side, or until the sweet potato is tender to the point of a knife and the jerk paste is crunchy and slightly charred.

3 Stir the chives into the yogurt along with some salt and pepper, then put into a small serving bowl.

4 Serve the sweet potato wedges at once while still sizzling hot, accompanied by the chive yogurt, wedges of lime and plenty of soft bread, if liked.

Quick yeasted herb & garlic flat bread ⓥ

This is a very easy bread that you both mix and let rise in the food processor! It couldn't be simpler.

SERVES 4
PREPARATION 20 MINUTES,
   PLUS RISING
COOKING 20–30 MINUTES

500 g (1 lb) strong white bread flour
1 packet fast-action dried yeast
2 teaspoons sea salt, plus extra
   for sprinkling
350 ml (12 fl oz) warm water
6 tablespoons olive oil
4 tablespoons chopped thyme
2 garlic cloves, crushed

1 Put the flour into a food processor fitted with a plastic dough blade. Add the yeast, the 2 teaspoons salt, the water and 2 tablespoons of the olive oil and pulse until a dough forms, then blend for 1 minute. Leave, with the lid on, for 45 minutes, or until the dough has doubled in size.

2 Add the thyme and garlic and process briefly to mix, then remove the dough from the machine, divide in half and press each into a wide 900 g (1 lb 13 oz) loaf tin or 20 cm (8 inch) square tin. Cover with clingfilm and leave for 1 hour to rise.

3 Press your fingers into the top of the bread a few times and drizzle the rest of the olive oil over the loaves and into the holes, then sprinkle with some sea salt.

4 Bake the loaves in a preheated oven, 200°C (400°F), Gas Mark 6, for 20–30 minutes, or until the loaves are golden brown on top and sound hollow when turned out of the tins and tapped on the base. (The timing will depend on the exact size of your tin – the deeper the dough in the tin, the longer it will take to cook.)

5 Cool on a wire rack, or wrap each loaf in a clean tea cloth and leave to cool slowly if you want the bread to have a soft crust.

Green olives with mixed peppercorns & coriander ⓥ

Why marinate your own olives when you can buy them? Because they're so easy to make yourself and you can rustle them up when you want them from storecupboard ingredients – but most of all, because these are divine!

SERVES 4

PREPARATION 10 MINUTES,
  PLUS MARINATING

340 g (11½ oz) can green queen
  olives in brine, drained
2 garlic cloves, finely sliced
1 lemon
1 tablespoon coriander seeds
1 tablespoon mixed peppercorns
  – black, white, green, pink and
  pimiento
extra virgin olive oil, for marinating

1 Put the olives into a bowl with the garlic. Cut thin strips of rind from half the lemon, using a zester if possible, and add to the olives. Slice the remaining half of the lemon thinly, then cut the slices into smaller pieces again and add to the bowl.

2 Crush the coriander seeds and peppercorns coarsely using a pestle and mortar or by putting them into a strong polythene bag and bashing with a rolling pin. Add to the bowl, then pour in enough olive oil to cover the olives and leave to marinate for at least 1 hour, or longer if there's time.

Desserts & cakes

White chocolate ice cream
with summer berry sauce

SERVES 6
PREPARATION 30 MINUTES,
    PLUS COOLING AND FREEZING
COOKING 10 MINUTES

2 eggs
275 ml (9 fl oz) single cream
125 g (3 oz) caster sugar
300 g (10 oz) white chocolate,
    broken into pieces
275 ml (9fl oz) double cream

FOR THE SAUCE

1 kg (2 lb) mixed summer berries, such
    as redcurrants, blackcurrants,
    blueberries, raspberries and
    blackberries
50–125 g (2–4 oz) caster sugar

1 To make the ice cream, whisk the eggs and sugar in a bowl. Pour the single cream into a saucepan, bring to the boil and pour over the eggs. Whisk, then pour the mixture back into the saucepan. Cook over a very gentle heat, stirring all the time, for a few minutes, until the mixture coats the back of the spoon very lightly. Remove from the heat and stir in the white chocolate. Cover and leave to cool, stirring from time to time to help the chocolate melt.

2 Whip the double cream until thick, then fold into the cooled chocolate mixture. Pour into a suitable container for freezing, put into the freezer and leave until solid, stirring a couple of times during the freezing process if possible. Alternatively, freeze in an ice-cream maker, following the manufacturer's instructions.

3 To make the sauce, put the fruit and 50 g (2 oz) sugar into a saucepan and heat gently until the juices run – this will take only a few minutes. Remove from the heat, taste and add more sugar to taste if necessary, remembering that the ice cream is quite sweet, so a sharpness in the sauce makes a pleasant contrast.

4 Remove the ice cream from the freezer about 30 minutes before you want to serve it to allow it to soften a little, then serve in scoops with the sauce.

Little lemon cheesecakes with blueberries

SERVES 6
PREPARATION 25 MINUTES

175 g (6 oz) ginger biscuits
75 g (3 oz) butter, melted
175 g (6 oz) blueberries
icing sugar, for dusting

TOPPING

400 g (13 oz) low-fat soft cream cheese
finely grated rind of 2 lemons
25 g (1 oz) caster sugar
150 ml (¼ pint) double cream
4 tablespoons lemon juice

1 Put the biscuits into a polythene bag, close the top, then crush with a rolling pin. Tip the crushed biscuits into a bowl, add the melted butter and mix to combine. Divide the mixture between 6 x 9–10 cm (3½–4 inch) round loose-based flan tins, pressing it on to the bases in an even layer (don't attempt to go up the sides). Place in the freezer or refrigerator while you make the topping.

2 If there is any liquid on top of the cream cheese, pour it away, then put the cheese into a bowl and add the lemon rind and sugar. Stir to make a creamy mixture, then add the cream and whisk until thick. Add the lemon juice and stir with a spoon – the acid in the juice will make the mixture even thicker.

3 Spoon the cream cheese mixture into the flan tins. Spread the mixture to the edges, but don't try to smooth the surface. Chill until required.

4 To finish, lift the little cheesecakes out of the tins – they will come out easily – and gently slide them on to individual plates, removing the bases of the tins as you do so. Decorate the tops with blueberries, dust with icing sugar and serve as soon as possible.

Whiskey cream banoffi

To make the toffee layer you need caramelized condensed milk. You can buy caramel condensed milk from most supermarkets or make it yourself with cans of plain condensed milk. You can caramelize more than one can at a time as long as they are all covered with water as described below. They will keep for months, enabling you to make this yummy pudding quickly.

SERVES 4–6

PREPARATION 20 MINUTES,
  PLUS COOLING AND CHILLING
COOKING 3–4 HOURS

400 g (13 oz) can caramel condensed milk or condensed milk
250 g (8 oz) digestive biscuits
125 g (4 oz) butter, melted
2–3 large bananas
300 ml (½ pint) double cream
4 tablespoons Baileys cream liqueur
25 g (1 oz) dark chocolate, grated

1 If using condensed milk, put the unopened can into a deep saucepan and add cold water to cover it by at least 5 cm (2 inches) – you can put the tin on its side if it fits better. Bring to the boil, then leave to simmer for 3–4 hours. Make sure you keep the water level topped up so that it's always at least 5 cm (2 inches) above the can (set a timer to remind you). This process is perfectly safe as long as you follow these instructions. Leave the can to cool in the water.

2 Put the biscuits in a large polythene bag, close the top, then crush with a rolling pin to make fine crumbs. Mix the biscuit crumbs with the melted butter, then press into the base of a 20–23 cm (8–9 inch) flan dish. If there's time, chill for 10–15 minutes.

3 Peel the bananas and slice each in half lengthways. Lay the slices of banana, cut-side down, in the flan case, cutting them as necessary to make them fit.

4 Spoon the caramelized condensed milk evenly over the bananas, to cover them.

5 Whip the cream with the Baileys until it forms soft peaks, then spoon on top of the caramel, taking it to the edges of the dish. Sprinkle grated chocolate all over the top. Chill until required – if anything, this tastes even better after 24 hours.

Mango, cardamom & pistachio fool

This is gorgeous, but for a less-rich version, use thick Greek yogurt, or half yogurt and half cream, whipped together.

SERVES 4
PREPARATION 15 MINUTES

½ teaspoon cardamom seeds
1 large ripe mango
300 ml (½ pint) double cream
2 tablespoons shelled pistachios, halved

1 Crush the cardamom seeds using a pestle and mortar, or the end of a rolling pin on a board, removing the outer husks. Set aside.

2 Make 2 cuts through the mango straight down about 5 mm (¼ inch) either side of the stalk, to cut the flesh from the flat stone. Peel off the skin and cut the flesh into rough pieces; remove as much flesh from around the stone as you can. Put all the mango flesh into a food processor, along with the cardamom, and whiz to a purée.

3 Whip the cream until it stands in stiff peaks, then gently fold in the mango purée, not too thoroughly, to give a pretty marbled effect. Spoon the mixture into 4 glasses and top with the pistachios.

Microwave-steamed maple syrup pudding

Once in a while it's nice to have a real indulgence and it's also fun to do some 'real' cooking in the microwave. I like to make this on a dreary winter's day, perhaps for Sunday lunch. It's so quick, you can do it on the spur of the moment.

SERVES 4
PREPARATION 20 MINUTES,
    PLUS STANDING
COOKING 10 MINUTES

175 g (6 oz) butter, softened
175 g (6 oz) caster sugar
6 tablespoons milk or milk and water
175 g (6 oz) self-raising flour
1½ teaspoons baking powder
3 eggs
5 tablespoons real maple syrup, plus
    extra to serve (optional)
toasted chopped walnuts, to decorate

1 Put the butter, sugar, milk, flour, baking powder, eggs and 1 tablespoon of the maple syrup into a food processor and whiz to a creamy consistency. Alternatively, put them into a bowl and beat with a wooden spoon or hand whisk until light and fluffy.

2 Pour the remaining maple syrup into the bottom of a lightly greased plastic 1.2 litre (2 pint) microwaveable pudding bowl, then spoon the sponge mixture on top.

3 Microwave, uncovered, until the sponge has risen and a skewer inserted into the centre comes out clean. This takes about 10 minutes in my microwave, which is 650w. You can cook it for a few minutes, then have a look and see how it's getting on – it won't spoil it.

4 Leave the pudding to stand for a few minutes, then turn out on to a warmed serving plate (or you could serve it straight from the bowl if you prefer), so that the golden syrupy top is uppermost, and decorate with the walnuts. Serve with extra maple syrup, if liked.

No microwave?
If you don't have a microwave, you can steam the sponge mixture, but leaving out the milk or water. Make a pleat in a piece of foil, place over the top and sides of the bowl and tie with string around the rim of the bowl – or, much easier, use a plastic bowl with a snap-on lid. Put the basin in a steamer fitted over a saucepan of boiling water and steam for 1½ hours, checking the level of the water from time to time and topping up with boiling water if necessary.

Cappuccino meringues

Meringues are a wonderful fat-free treat and easy to make; the filling can be as indulgent or virtuous as you like.

MAKES 12 HALVES
PREPARATION 15 MINUTES
COOKING 2 HOURS

2 egg whites
1 teaspoon good-quality instant coffee granules
125 g (4 oz) caster sugar

FOR THE FILLING

150 ml (¼ pint) fromage frais, low-fat crème fraîche or thick Greek yogurt
drinking chocolate powder, for dusting

1 Line a baking sheet with nonstick baking paper.

2 Put the egg whites and instant coffee granules into a large, clean, grease-free bowl and whisk until very thick – the peaks formed must be able to hold their shape and you should be able to turn the bowl upside down without the mixture coming out. However, don't get it to the point where the whisked eggs start to break up and lose their volume. Add the sugar a tablespoon at a time, whisking after each addition.

3 Put heaped dessertspoonfuls of the mixture on to the baking paper, leaving a little space between them. Bake in a preheated oven, 120°C (250°F), Gas Mark ½, for 2 hours, until they have dried out. If possible, switch off the heat and leave them in the oven to get completely cold.

4 To finish the meringues, sandwich pairs together with a good spoonful of your chosen filling, put on a plate and dust with a little chocolate powder. Eat within about 2 hours.

Vanilla-poached figs ⓥ

A wonderful way to turn less-than-perfect figs into a plump, succulent treat. The vanilla pods can be used again. Remove them after use, rinse under the tap and leave to dry. A good way to store them is buried in a jar of caster sugar; this absorbs their flavour and keeps them dry.

SERVES 4
PREPARATION 10 MINUTES
COOKING 30 MINUTES

450 ml (¾ pint) water
3 tablespoons caster sugar
2 vanilla pods
8 fresh figs
250 g (8 oz) thick natural yogurt,
   to serve (optional)

1 Make a light syrup: put the water, sugar and vanilla pods into a saucepan large enough to take the figs, bring to the boil and simmer for 5 minutes.

2 Add the figs to the pan. Bring to the boil, then cover and cook over a gentle heat for 20 minutes, or until the figs are plump and very tender when pierced with the point of a sharp knife.

3 Remove the figs from the pan with a slotted spoon. In each fig, make a cut lengthways, almost to the bottom of the fruit, then another cut perpendicular to it. Place in a shallow serving dish. Boil the syrup and vanilla pods hard for a few minutes until it has reduced a little and thickened. Pour the syrup over the figs. Serve hot, warm or cold, with natural yogurt, if liked.

Chilli kulfi

SERVES 4

PREPARATION 15 MINUTES,
   PLUS STANDING, COOLING AND
   FREEZING

COOKING 5 MINUTES

750 ml (1¼ pints) single cream
¼ teaspoon dried red chilli flakes
10 cardamom pods, crushed
a good pinch of saffron threads
   (optional)
175 g (6 oz) caster sugar
2 teaspoons rosewater
25 g (1 oz) ground almonds
25 g (1 oz) chopped pistachio nuts
a few fresh rose petals or extra
   pistachios, to decorate

1 Put the cream into a saucepan with the chilli flakes, cardamom pods and saffron, if using. Bring to the boil, then remove from the heat, cover and leave to stand for 10–15 minutes for the flavours to infuse.

2 Strain the mixture into a bowl and add the sugar, stirring until it dissolves. Stir in the rosewater, ground almonds and pistachio nuts and leave to cool.

3 Line 4 x 150 ml (¼ pint) individual pudding basins, ramekins or disposable cups with clingfilm, then pour in the cooled kulfi mixture, dividing it evenly between them, and freeze until solid.

4 Remove the kulfi from the freezer about 15 minutes before you want to serve them. Turn them out of the containers on to dishes, peel off the clingfilm and serve, scattered with a few fresh rose petals if available or extra pistachios.

Espresso risotto

Whenever possible, I prefer to use soya milk instead of cows' milk. Soya milk is healthy for us and it gives a very creamy flavour to this risotto as well as to sauces. This is also good cold, with the whipped cream folded in.

SERVES 4

PREPARATION 10 MINUTES,
  PLUS STANDING

COOKING 35–40 MINUTES

125 g (4 oz) risotto or pudding rice
150 ml (¼ pint) water
1 tablespoon good-quality strong
  instant coffee granules
600 ml (1 pint) soya milk
25 g (1 oz) unsalted butter
2 tablespoons rum
150 ml (¼ pint) double cream,
  lightly whipped
1–2 tablespoons coffee sugar crystals,
  to decorate (optional)

1 Put the rice and water into a medium-sized saucepan, bring to the boil and simmer for 5 minutes.

2 Add the coffee granules and soya milk. Bring to the boil, then leave to boil away gently for 20–30 minutes, stirring often, until the rice is tender and the mixture quite thick.

3 Remove from the heat, add the butter and rum, cover and leave to stand for 10 minutes, or until ready to serve.

4 Serve into warmed individual bowls, top each with a generous spoonful of whipped cream and a scattering of coffee sugar granules, if liked – or hand the cream and the sugar separately.

Honey & ginger pashka
with bitter chocolate sauce

SERVES 4
PREPARATION 10 MINUTES,
   PLUS OVERNIGHT CHILLING
COOKING 5 MINUTES

50 g (2 oz) unsalted butter, softened
4 tablespoons thick honey
500 g (1 lb) ricotta cheese
grated rind of 1 orange and 1 lemon
½ teaspoon vanilla extract
50 g (2 oz) candied orange or
   lemon peel, chopped
50 g (2 oz) preserved ginger in syrup,
   drained and chopped
50 g (2 oz) toasted flaked almonds
a few edible fresh flowers, to decorate
   (optional)

FOR THE SAUCE

100 g (3½ oz) bitter chocolate,
   broken into pieces
75 ml (3 fl oz) water

1 Line the inside of a clean plastic flowerpot, measuring 15 cm (6 inches) across the top, with pieces of baking paper.

2 Put the butter into a food processor or large bowl with 2 tablespoons of the honey, the ricotta, citrus rinds and vanilla extract and blend together, then stir in the candied peel, ginger and half the almonds.

3 Spoon the mixture into the flowerpot and level the surface. Stand the flowerpot in a bowl – to catch the liquid that will leak out – and leave in the refrigerator for 12–24 hours.

4 Just before you want to serve the pashka, make the sauce by melting together the chocolate and the water in a small saucepan over a gentle heat.

5 To serve, invert the flowerpot over a plate – the pashka will slide out easily and you can then peel off the paper. Quickly heat the remaining honey in a small saucepan and pour over the top of the pashka to make a glaze, which will run down the sides. Top with the remaining almonds and decorate the base with a few fresh flowers, if you like. Serve with the chocolate sauce in a small jug or bowl.

Coconut & honey ice cream with banana-sesame fritters

SERVES 4
PREPARATION 10 MINUTES,
  PLUS FREEZING
COOKING 35 MINUTES

400 ml (14 fl oz) can coconut milk
3 tablespoons thick honey
300 ml (½ pint) double cream
lime wedges, to serve

FOR THE BANANA FRITTERS

125 g (4 oz) self-raising flour
2 teaspoons caster sugar
175 ml (6 fl oz) water
rapeseed oil, for deep- or shallow-
  frying
2 large bananas, cut into 1 cm
  (½ inch) diagonal slices
25 g (1 oz) sesame seeds

1 First make the ice cream. Put the coconut milk into a bowl and whisk to remove lumps, then whisk in the honey and cream. Pour into a suitable container for freezing, put into the freezer and leave until firm, whisking it a couple of times during the freezing process. Alternatively, freeze in an ice-cream maker, following the manufacturer's instructions.

2 Remove the ice cream from the freezer 30 minutes or so before you want to serve it to allow it to soften a little.

3 To make the fritters, put the flour and sugar into a bowl and gradually stir in the water to make a coating batter.

4 Heat the rapeseed oil in a deep-fat fryer until a few drops of the batter when added to the pan sizzle and rise immediately to the surface of the oil. Dip slices of banana in the batter, then slide into the hot oil – don't add too many at a time. Fry until the batter is crisp and golden brown, then remove the fritters with a slotted spoon, drain on kitchen paper and scatter with the sesame seeds.

5 Continue until all the fritters are done, then serve immediately, with wedges of lime and accompanied by scoops of the coconut ice cream.

Honeydew melon, strawberry & mint compôte ⓥ

You can't tell by its scent whether a honeydew melon is ripe so buy from a reputable supplier in July or August to be sure of one with succulent, sweet and melting flesh.

SERVES 4
PREPARATION 15 MINUTES,
  PLUS STANDING

20 g (¾ oz) mint leaves
75 g (3 oz) caster sugar or clear honey
1 ripe honeydew melon
500 g (1 lb) strawberries, hulled
  and sliced

1 Put the mint leaves into a large bowl and crush lightly with the end of a rolling pin or a wooden spoon. Add the sugar or honey and crush the leaves again by pressing them against the side of the bowl with a wooden spoon. Set aside.

2 Halve the melon, scoop out and discard the seeds. Scoop out the flesh with a melon-baller, or simply use a sharp knife to cut it away from the skin and into bite-sized pieces.

3 Put the melon into a bowl with the mint and add the strawberries. Stir, then cover and leave for 1–4 hours for the flavours to blend. The fruit compôte will produce its own liquid and is deliciously refreshing served cold, but not icy.

Spicy vegan carrot cake Ⓥ

SERVES 4
PREPARATION 20 MINUTES
COOKING 1¼ HOURS

250 g (8 oz) scraped carrots, grated
125 g (4 oz) raisins
6 tablespoons rapeseed or olive oil
125 g (4 oz) unrefined cane sugar
250 g (8 oz) self-raising flour
1 teaspoon grated nutmeg
1 teaspoon ground cinnamon
8 tablespoons apple juice concentrate
   (available from healthfood shops)
   or real maple syrup
4 tablespoons orange juice

FOR THE FROSTING

200 g (7 oz) dairy-free alternative
   to soft cheese
grated rind of 1 orange
25 g (1 oz) caster sugar
strands of orange rind, to decorate

1 Line a 20 cm (8 inch) square cake tin with nonstick baking paper.

2 Put the carrots, raisins, rapeseed or olive oil and cane sugar into a bowl and mix. Add the flour, nutmeg, cinnamon, apple and orange juices and mix again until everything is combined – the mixture will be quite sticky.

3 Spoon the mixture into the prepared cake tin and level the surface. Bake in a preheated oven, 160°C (325°F), Gas Mark 3, for 1¼ hours, or until a skewer inserted into the centre comes out clean. Leave in the tin until completely cold.

4 To make the frosting, mix the dairy-free alternative to soft cheese with the orange rind and caster sugar, then spread over the top of the cold cake. Decorate with strands of orange rind.

Grilled pineapple with palm sugar & crème fraîche

The pineapple can be cooked under a hot grill, but the very nicest way to do it is on a barbecue at the end of the main cooking, when the embers are dying down – it makes a lovely end to an al fresco meal.

SERVES 4
PREPARATION 10 MINUTES
COOKING 10 MINUTES

1 large ripe juicy pineapple
neutral-tasting oil, such as rapeseed
   or light olive oil, for brushing
175 g (6 oz) palm sugar, chopped
   if in a solid block
300 ml (½ pint) crème fraîche, to
   serve

1 Cut the pineapple lengthways through the leaves, first in half, then into sixths or eighths, depending on the size of the pineapple – it's best if the wedges are no more than about 1 cm (½ inch) thick. Brush them all over with the cooking oil.

2 Put the pineapple slices on a grill pan and cook under a preheated grill, or cook on a barbecue grid. Cook for about 10 minutes in all, turning them halfway through cooking when the first side is tender and, if on a grid, attractively marked by it. Remove from the heat and sprinkle with palm sugar.

3 Serve the pineapple with bowls of the crème fraîche and palm sugar for people to help themselves.

Melting chocolate puddings

Little melting chocolate puddings have become a modern classic – and these provide a new twist because when you cut them open, white chocolate oozes out! They are easy to do and can be prepared well in advance, ready for cooking just before serving.

SERVES 4
PREPARATION 25 MINUTES
COOKING 20 MINUTES

50 g (2 oz) butter, plus extra
    for greasing
100 g (3½ oz) plain chocolate, broken
    into pieces
2 eggs
50 g (2 oz) caster sugar
½ teaspoon vanilla extract
1 tablespoon plain white flour
8 squares, 25–50 g (1–2 oz),
    good-quality white chocolate
cocoa powder, for dusting
thick cream, to serve

1 Line the bases of 4 x 150 ml (¼ pint) individual metal pudding basins with circles of nonstick baking paper, then butter them very thoroughly.

2 Melt the plain chocolate and butter in a heatproof bowl set over a pan of gently steaming water. Stir, remove from the heat and leave to cool slightly.

3 Using an electric whisk, beat together the eggs, sugar and vanilla extract until very thick and pale – this takes at least 5 minutes.

4 Gently fold the melted chocolate and flour into the whisked mixture until completely incorporated. Put 1 tablespoon of the chocolate mixture into each pudding basin and place in a preheated oven, 200°C (400°F), Gas Mark 6, for 5 minutes, then remove them and quickly fill the basins with the rest of the mixture. Drop 2 squares of the white chocolate into each. Put them back into the oven and bake for 11–12 minutes, or until risen and a bit crusty around the edges.

5 Remove from the oven and leave to stand for 1–2 minutes, then slip a knife around the sides and invert each pudding over a warmed plate. Leave for another 30 seconds, then gently lift off the pudding basins. Dust the puddings with a little cocoa powder and serve immediately with thick cream.

Little plum upside-down puddings
with cinnamon custard

Chef's rings are ideal for making these, but if you don't have any, you could use 10 cm (4 inch) loose-based shallow flan tins lined with circles of nonstick baking paper.

SERVES 4
PREPARATION 30 MINUTES
COOKING 30 MINUTES

butter, for greasing
125 g (4 oz) caster sugar, plus extra
   to taste
500 g (1 lb) plums, stoned and sliced
4 tablespoons water

FOR THE SPONGE

2 eggs
50 g (2 oz) caster sugar
50 g (2 oz) self-raising flour

FOR THE CUSTARD

2 egg yolks
1 teaspoon cornflour
1 tablespoon caster sugar
300 ml (½ pint) creamy milk
½ cinnamon stick

1 Line a baking sheet with nonstick baking paper, grease generously with butter and place 4 x 10 cm (4 inch) chef's metal rings on it. Sprinkle inside the rings lightly with some of the sugar.

2 Put the plums into a saucepan with the rest of the sugar and the water. Cover and cook over a moderate heat for 3–4 minutes, or until the plums are just tender but not collapsed. Remove from the heat. Taste and add more sugar if necessary.

3 To make the sponge, whisk the eggs and sugar together until very thick and pale – this takes about 5 minutes with an electric whisk. Sift the flour over the top and fold in gently with a spatula.

4 Divide the plums between the rings, spreading them out so that they cover the whole area. Spoon the sponge mixture on top, levelling it off. Bake in a preheated oven, 180°C (350°F), Gas Mark 4, for 20 minutes, or until the sponge springs back when touched lightly in the centre.

5 To make the custard, put the egg yolks, cornflour and sugar into a bowl and whisk together. Pour the milk into a saucepan, add the cinnamon stick and bring to the boil. Gradually whisk the hot milk into the egg mixture, then return the mixture to the pan and stir over a gentle heat for a few minutes until the mixture thickens and will coat the back of a spoon. Remove the cinnamon stick. The custard can be served hot or cold.

6 Run a knife around the edges of the rings, then turn each pudding out on to a warmed serving plate. Pour a little of the custard around, and serve the rest in a jug.

Pear & brioche charlotte

SERVES 4

PREPARATION 25 MINUTES, PLUS
  COOLING

COOKING 1¼ HOURS

750 g (1½ lb) pears, peeled, cored
  and cut into pieces
2 tablespoons caster sugar
2 tablespoons water
1 vanilla pod
8–10 slices of brioche
125 g (4 oz) butter, melted
250 g (8 oz) mascarpone cheese
2 egg yolks
2 tablespoons demerara sugar
thick pouring cream, to serve
  (optional)

1 Put the pears into a saucepan with the caster sugar, water and vanilla pod. Bring to the boil, then reduce the heat, cover and leave to cook very gently for about 30 minutes, or until the pears are very tender. Leave until completely cold.

2 Brush the slices of brioche with the melted butter and arrange them in a 20 cm (8 inch) sponge sandwich cake tin with a removable base, or a shallow ovenproof casserole, covering the base and sides and saving some slices for the top.

3 Beat the mascarpone a little to soften. Mix in the egg yolks and the pears together with any liquid. Spoon this on top of the brioche, then put the remaining brioche slices on top, brush with melted butter and sprinkle with demerara sugar.

4 Bake in a preheated oven, 180°C (350°F), Gas Mark 4, for about 40 minutes, or until the charlotte is golden, crisp and set in the middle – cover it with a piece of foil towards the end of the cooking time if it seems to be getting too crisp on top before the inside is set.

5 Serve hot, warm or cold, with pouring cream, if you like.

Banana & Earl Grey cake

The bergamot oil, which you can get at any healthfood shop, intensifies the flavour of the Earl Grey in this stylish cake.

SERVES 4
PREPARATION 10 MINUTES,
  PLUS STANDING
COOKING 30–35 MINUTES

8 Earl Grey tea bags
250 ml (8 fl oz) boiling water
1 large banana
125 g (4 oz) butter, softened
125 g (4 oz) soft brown sugar
2 eggs
200 g (7 oz) self-raising flour
2 teaspoons baking powder

FOR THE ICING

175 g (6 oz) icing sugar
1 teaspoon butter
1 drop of bergamot essential oil
  (optional)

1 Add the tea bags to the boiling water in a measuring jug, making sure they're all submerged. Cover with a plate and leave until cold.

2 Squeeze the tea bags to get as much liquid from them as possible, then discard the tea bags and measure out 150 ml (¼ pint) tea. Put this tea into a food processor or mixer (reserve the rest). Peel and mash the banana and add to the tea with the butter, soft brown sugar, eggs, flour and baking powder, then whiz or beat until the mixture is light and fluffy.

3 Line an 18–20 cm (7–8 inch) cake tin with nonstick baking paper. Spoon the mixture into the tin and gently level the surface. Bake in a preheated oven, 180°C (350°F), Gas Mark 4, for 30–35 minutes, or until a skewer inserted into the centre comes out clean. Cool for a minute or so in the tin, then turn out on to a wire rack and leave until cold.

4 To make the icing, put the icing sugar into a saucepan with the butter, bergamot oil, if using, and 2 tablespoons of the remaining tea. Stir over the heat until the butter has melted. Pour over the top of the cake and leave to set.

Lemon & almond drizzle cake with berries

SERVES 4
PREPARATION 25 MINUTES,
   PLUS STANDING
COOKING 40–45 MINUTES

175 g (6 oz) butter, softened
175 g (6 oz) caster sugar
2 eggs
finely grated rind of 1 lemon
175 g (6 oz) self-raising flour
50 g (2 oz) ground almonds
1½ teaspoons baking powder
crème fraîche, to serve

FOR THE DRIZZLE TOPPING

4 tablespoons lemon juice
150 g (5 oz) icing sugar

FOR THE BERRIES

500 g (1 lb) mixed berries, such
   as raspberries, strawberries,
   blueberries or redcurrants,
   any stems and hulls
   removed
caster sugar, to taste

1 Line a 900 g (1 lb 13 oz) loaf tin with a strip of nonstick baking paper to cover the base and narrow sides.

2 Put the butter, caster sugar, eggs, lemon rind, flour, ground almonds and baking powder into a bowl and beat together until creamy.

3 Spoon the mixture into the prepared loaf tin and gently level the surface. Bake in a preheated oven, 160°C (325°F), Gas Mark 3, for 40–45 minutes, until risen and firm to a light touch and a skewer inserted into the centre comes out clean.

4 Five minutes before the cake is done, make the drizzle topping. Mix the lemon juice and icing sugar in a small saucepan, then stir over a gentle heat until the icing sugar has dissolved.

5 As soon as the cake comes out of the oven, prick the top all over and pour the icing sugar mixture over the top. Leave to cool, then remove the cake from the tin and strip off the paper.

6 Prepare the fruit an hour or so before you want to eat. Put it into a bowl, sprinkle over caster sugar to taste and leave to stand for 1 hour, stirring from time to time. Taste and add a little more sugar if necessary. Serve the fruit and cake with a bowl of crème fraîche.

Fig tarte tatin with ginger cream

This is also delicious made with apricots. Make exactly as described, using 900 g (1 lb 13 oz) apricots, halved and stoned, instead of the figs.

SERVES 4
PREPARATION 25 MINUTES
COOKING 30 MINUTES

325 g (11 oz) frozen ready-rolled
    all-butter puff pastry (see page 295)
40 g (1½ oz) butter
900 g (1 lb 13 oz) figs, halved
40 g (1½ oz) caster sugar
25 g (1 oz) toasted flaked almonds
    (optional)

FOR THE GINGER CREAM

275 ml (9 fl oz) double cream
3 pieces of preserved stem ginger,
    very finely chopped

1 Roll the pastry a little on a floured surface to make it a bit thinner if you can, then cut a circle to fit 1 cm (½ inch) larger than the top of a 20 cm (8 inch) tarte tatin pan or cake tin.

2 Melt the butter in the tarte tatin pan or in a frying pan. Add the figs, cut-side down, and the sugar. Cook over a high heat for about 6 minutes, until the figs are slightly browned and caramelized.

3 If you're using a cake tin, put the figs, cut-side down, into it and scrape in all the gooey juice from the pan.

4 Put the pastry on top, tucking it down into the figs at the sides. Prick the pastry, then bake in a preheated oven, 200°C (400°F), Gas Mark 6, for 20–25 minutes, until crisp and golden brown.

5 Meanwhile, make the ginger cream. Whip the cream until it forms soft peaks, then fold in the ginger. Transfer the cream to a bowl and chill until required.

6 To serve, loosen the tarte with a knife, then invert over a plate. The figs will be on top. Scatter with the almonds, if using, then leave to settle for a couple of minutes before serving with the ginger cream.

Individual pavlovas with pomegranate & grenadine

SERVES 4
PREPARATION 15 MINUTES,
  PLUS STANDING
COOKING 40 MINUTES

2 egg whites
125 g (4 oz) caster sugar
1 teaspoon cornflour
¼ teaspoon vinegar

FOR THE FILLING

2 ripe pomegranates
4 tablespoons grenadine
300 ml (½ pint) double cream,
  whipped

1 Line a large baking sheet with nonstick baking paper.

2 Put the egg whites into a large, clean, grease-free bowl and whisk until they are thick, glossy and standing in peaks. Add the sugar a tablespoon at a time, whisking after each addition, then fold in the cornflour and vinegar.

3 Spoon the mixture on to the baking paper, making 4 saucer-sized circles, and hollow each out in the centre a little. Bake in a preheated oven, 140°C (275°F), Gas Mark 1, for about 40 minutes, or until crisp on the outside but still soft within. Cool on the baking sheet. If possible, switch off the heat and leave in the oven to get completely cold.

4 While the pavlovas are cooking, cut the pomegranate in half and bend back the skin – as if you were turning it inside out – to make the seeds pop out. Put the pomegranate seeds into a small bowl with the grenadine and leave to steep.

5 To finish the pavlovas, spoon some whipped cream on to each, then top with the pomegranate seeds and their juice. Serve as soon as possible.

Fruit sushi plate ⓥ

A plate of sweet sushi rice and lemon grass-scented fruits makes a very pretty and refreshing dessert.

SERVES 4
PREPARATION 20 MINUTES,
   PLUS COOLING
COOKING 25 MINUTES

FOR THE RICE

175 g (6 oz) Japanese sushi rice
   or white pudding rice
50 g (2 oz) caster sugar
400 g (13 oz) can organic
   coconut milk
1 vanilla pod
juice of 1 lime

FOR THE FRUIT

125 g (4 oz) caster sugar
100 ml (3½ fl oz) water
1 lemon grass stalk, crushed
½ teaspoon dried red chilli flakes
juice and pared rind of 1 lime
1 carambola, thinly sliced
1 large ripe papaya, peeled, deseeded
   and sliced
2 kiwi fruits, peeled and sliced

1 Put the rice and sugar into a saucepan with the coconut milk and vanilla pod. Bring to the boil, then reduce the heat, cover and leave to cook very gently for 20 minutes, or until the rice is tender and the liquid has been absorbed. Remove from the heat, gently stir in the lime juice and leave to cool.

2 Meanwhile, make an aromatic syrup for the fruit. Put the sugar and water in a saucepan with the lemon grass, chilli flakes and lime rind. Heat gently until the sugar has dissolved, then bring to the boil and remove from the heat.

3 Put the carambola in a single layer on a plate and pour the hot syrup over, together with the lemon grass and lime rind. Cover and leave until cold, then remove the lemon grass and lime rind, squeeze them to extract all the flavour and discard them. Sprinkle over the lime juice.

4 To serve, form the sweet sushi rice into small circles 2 cm (¾ inch) in diameter and 1 cm (½ inch) thick and arrange on plates. Top with carambola, papaya and kiwi fruit slices and spoon the syrup over them. Serve the remaining fruit on the side.

Nectarines roasted with lavender ⓥ

The wonderful taste of summer on a plate – and so easy to do.

SERVES 4
PREPARATION 10 MINUTES
COOKING 25 MINUTES

40 g (1½ oz) butter
3 tablespoons demerara sugar
2–3 dried heads of lavender
6 nectarines, halved and stoned
chilled Greek yogurt, to serve

1 Select a shallow casserole dish that will hold all the nectarine halves in a single layer, grease generously with half the butter and sprinkle with half the sugar and half the lavender.

2 Place the nectarine halves, cut-side down, in the buttered casserole, dot with the rest of the butter and sprinkle with the remaining sugar and lavender.

3 Bake, uncovered, in a preheated oven, 180°C (350°F), Gas Mark 4, for about 25 minutes, or until the nectarines are tender. Serve hot or warm, with some chilled Greek yogurt.

Orange creams with caramel & toffee sauce

This is a great mixture of flavours and textures. The orange creams can be topped with crisp, shiny golden caramel if you have a cook's blowtorch, or you can place them under the grill – either way, they're delectable.

SERVES 4
PREPARATION 30 MINUTES,
   PLUS COOLING AND CHILLING
COOKING 45 MINUTES

FOR THE ORANGE CREAMS

300 ml (½ pint) double cream
2 pieces of pared orange rind
6 egg yolks
75 g (3 oz) caster sugar

FOR THE ORANGES

4 ripe sweet juicy oranges
caster sugar, to taste

FOR THE TOFFEE SAUCE

50 g (2 oz) butter
5 tablespoons double cream
4 tablespoons soft brown sugar

1 Line the bases of 4 ramekins with circles of nonstick baking paper.

2 To make the orange creams, put the cream and orange rind into a saucepan and bring to the boil. Remove from the heat and leave to cool slightly. Remove the orange rind.

3 Whisk together the egg yolks and 25 g (1 oz) of the caster sugar to blend, then gradually whisk in the cream. Pour the mixture into the prepared ramekins, stand them in a roasting tin and pour in boiling water to come half to three-quarters of the way up the sides of the ramekins. Bake in a preheated oven, 140°C (275°F), Gas Mark 1, for about 30 minutes, or until the custards are just firm in the centres. Remove from the oven, cool, then chill.

4 Cut the skin and pith from the oranges, then cut the segments out of the white inner skin. Put the segments into a bowl with a little caster sugar to taste if necessary and chill until required.

5 For the sauce, put the butter, cream and soft brown sugar into a saucepan and heat gently for 2–3 minutes, to make a golden toffee sauce.

6 To serve, loosen the sides of the orange creams and turn out on to plates, then remove the lining paper. Top each with a thin layer of the remaining caster sugar and heat with a cook's blowtorch to make a hard, glazed golden topping. Alternatively, turn them out on to a heatproof plate that will fit under your grill, top each with a thin layer of caster sugar and grill them for 1–2 minutes to make the caramel, then carefully transfer each to a serving plate. Arrange some orange slices on each plate and drizzle some toffee sauce around the oranges. Serve at once.

Pink Champagne granita marbled with raspberries ⓥ

This recipe makes the most wonderful ending to a special meal. You probably won't need all the granita – it might be called for as second helpings and it makes a wonderful pick-me-up for the cook (or anyone else!) the morning after, perhaps with some freshly squeezed pink grapefruit juice added. Incidentally, ordinary Champagne, rather than pink, is also great to use, but not as pretty.

SERVES 4

PREPARATION 15 MINUTES,
    PLUS COOLING AND FREEZING

COOKING 5 MINUTES

200 ml (7 fl oz) water
225 g (7½ oz) caster sugar, plus
    2 tablespoons
1 bottle pink Champagne
375 g (12 oz) raspberries

1 Put the water into a saucepan with the 225 g (7½ oz) sugar. Heat gently until the sugar has dissolved, then bring to the boil and remove from the heat. Leave to cool.

2 Mix the cooled sugar syrup with the Champagne. Pour into a shallow container so that the mixture is about 1 cm (½ inch) deep and put into the freezer, stirring the mixture from time to time as it becomes frozen around the edges. Because of the alcohol in the Champagne, it will take up to 4 hours to freeze, and will never become rock hard, so can be used straight from the freezer. It's fine to make it the day before needed.

3 To serve, first toss the raspberries in the remaining sugar and set aside for a few minutes until the sugar has dissolved. Put the raspberries into 4 serving glasses. Give the granita a quick stir with a fork, then scrape some into the glasses, on top of the raspberries and serve immediately.

Affogato with almond tuiles

This is an easy-to-make yet wonderful ice cream. Although freshly brewed espresso is the perfect topping for this – whisper it quietly, instant espresso is also fine: by the time it has mixed with the ice cream, I defy anyone to tell the difference!

SERVES 4
PREPARATION 30 MINUTES, PLUS
   FREEZING
COOKING 15–20 MINUTES

600 ml (1 pint) double or
   whipping cream
400 g (13 oz) can skimmed
   condensed milk
150 ml (¼ pint) strong espresso coffee

FOR THE ALMOND TUILES

1 egg white
50 g (2 oz) caster sugar
25 g (1 oz) plain white flour, sifted
25 g (1 oz) butter, melted
40 g (1½ oz) flaked almonds
flavourless vegetable oil, such as
   grapeseed, for greasing

1 To make the ice cream, whisk the cream until it forms soft peaks. Add the condensed milk to the cream and whisk again until combined. Tip into a suitable container for freezing, put into the freezer and leave until firm.

2 To make the tuiles, line a large baking sheet with nonstick baking paper. Whisk the egg white until stiff, then whisk in the sugar. Add the flour and butter alternately to make a smooth mixture. Place big teaspoons of the mixture well apart on the baking paper (you'll probably get about 4 to a large sheet) and, using the back of the spoon, spread the mixture out to make rounds each about 10 cm (4 inches) in diameter. Sprinkle the top of each with the almonds, then bake in a preheated oven, 180°C (350°F), Gas Mark 4, for 4–5 minutes, until set and lightly browned, especially around the edges.

3 Remove from the oven and leave to cool for a minute or so until firm enough to lift from the baking sheet. Meanwhile, oil a rolling pin. Drape the tuiles over the rolling pin so that as they cool they become curved. Once they're cool they can be removed to a wire rack.

4 Continue with the rest of the mixture to make about 16 tuiles. When they're all cold, store in a tin until required.

5 To serve, scoop the ice cream into 4 bowls. Pour a couple of tablespoons of the hot coffee over each and serve immediately, with the tuiles.

White chocolate gelato with citrus drizzle

Because of its light consistency – made mainly with milk rather than cream – gelato takes longer to freeze than normal ice cream and for this reason I find it best to use the freezer rather than an ice-cream maker. Having said that, this gelato couldn't be simpler to make.

SERVES 4
PREPARATION 15 MINUTES,
   PLUS COOLING AND FREEZING
COOKING 15 MINUTES

750 ml (1¼ pints) milk
2 x 150 g (5 oz) bars white chocolate,
   broken into pieces
1½ teaspoons cornflour
125 ml (4 fl oz) double cream

FOR THE CITRUS DRIZZLE
juice and finely grated rind of 1 orange
juice and finely grated rind of 1 lime
100 g (3½ oz) caster sugar

1 To make the ice cream, put the milk into a saucepan and bring to the boil. Remove from the heat and stir in the chocolate.

2 Put the cornflour in a small bowl with some of the cream and blend to a smooth paste. Reheat the chocolate milk, then tip it into the cornflour mixture, stir and return it to the saucepan, along with the rest of the cream. Bring to the boil, stir for a minute or so until it thickens, then remove from the heat and leave to cool.

3 Pour the cooled mixture into a suitable container for freezing, put into the freezer and leave until solid, stirring from time to time during the freezing process if possible.

4 To make the citrus drizzle, put the orange and lime juices and rinds into a small saucepan with the sugar and gently bring to the boil. Reduce the heat and simmer for about 5 minutes until reduced in quantity and slightly thickened (watch carefully as it burns easily). Set aside until required.

5 To serve, remove the ice cream from the freezer about 30 minutes before you want to serve it to soften a little, then scoop into bowls. Check the citrus drizzle: if it has become very thick, lighten it a bit by stirring in a teaspoon or so of hot water. Then swirl some citrus drizzle over the top of each portion and serve at once.

Chocolate truffles

These heavenly truffles have rich, creamy centres like Belgian chocolates and are absolutely worth the effort.

MAKES ABOUT 22
PREPARATION 30 MINUTES,
   PLUS CHILLING
COOKING 5 MINUTES

FOR THE WHITE CHOCOLATE AND COFFEE TRUFFLES

100 g (3½ oz) white chocolate, broken into pieces
25 g (1 oz) cold unsalted butter, cut into small pieces
75 ml (3 fl oz) cold double cream
½ teaspoon instant espresso coffee
1 teaspoon boiling water
100 g (3½ oz) melted white chocolate, sifted cocoa powder or finely ground toasted hazelnuts, to coat

FOR THE MILK CHOCOLATE TRUFFLES WITH SOFT CENTRES

100 g (3½ oz) milk chocolate, broken into pieces
25 g (1 oz) cold unsalted butter, cut into small pieces
2 tablespoons cold double cream
1 teaspoon brandy (optional)
150 g (5 oz) melted milk chocolate, sifted cocoa powder or finely ground toasted hazelnuts, to coat

1 To make the white chocolate and coffee truffles, melt the white chocolate in a heatproof bowl set over a pan of gently steaming water. Take the bowl off the heat and stir in first the butter and then the cream. Dissolve the coffee in the boiling water and stir into the mixture, then chill in the refrigerator until firm – about 1 hour.

2 Divide the white chocolate mixture into 10 even-sized pieces and form into balls. Place these on nonstick baking paper and put into the freezer to chill thoroughly for about 1 hour.

3 To coat with chocolate, dip the frozen chocolates into the melted white chocolate – it will set very quickly – coating both sides. Alternatively, roll the truffles in cocoa powder or finely ground toasted hazelnuts. Put them on nonstick baking paper and chill in the refrigerator until required.

4 To make the milk chocolate truffles, melt the 100 g (3½ oz) milk chocolate in a heatproof bowl as before, then remove from the heat and beat in the butter, cream and brandy, if using. Chill in the refrigerator until fairly firm, then proceed as described for the white truffles, using milk chocolate, cocoa powder or nuts to coat.

5 Store all the truffles in the refrigerator until required.

Notes on ingredients

Almond butter Available with no added ingredients such as emulsifiers, from good healthfood shops. There is a brown version and a white one. The oil may separate in the jar – just give it a good stir before use.

Arame seaweed A delicately flavoured seaweed, available dried from good healthfood shops. Simply wash and soak briefly before use.

Bergamot oil An essential oil, a small quantity of which can be used as a flavouring; available from healthfood shops.

Buckwheat Strictly speaking, a seed, though usually classified as a grain. Available from organic food shops, raw or toasted. I prefer to buy raw and, if required, toast it briefly in a dry pan before use.

Caster sugar I like to use Fair Trade golden caster sugar (and other ingredients) when available. Golden caster sugar is not much different in flavour and nutritional content to the white stuff, but I find it more aesthetically pleasing!

Coconut milk Organic coconut milk is much nicer than the non-organic type (which has unnecessary additives) and there's no point in buying the low-fat version as it's just coconut milk with water added – you might as well buy the whole type and add your own water.

Curry leaves Can be found in some large supermarkets and Indian food shops. They freeze well, so it's worth buying up a good supply of fresh ones when you see them – just pop them into the freezer and use when required.

Daikon A large tapered white radish with a slightly hot flavour, available from supermarkets and Asian shops. Turnip can be substituted.

Eggs Use free-range, preferably organic, eggs.

Epazote A herb with a pungent, savoury flavour, often used in Mexican bean recipes to make the beans less wind-inducing. Dried epazote can be found in Mexican shops. The herb savory, which is said to have the same effect, can be substituted, or mixed herbs can be used for flavour.

Garam masala A mixture of ground spices added towards the end of cooking to enhance the flavour. Every keen Indian cook has their own recipe, made from spices that they roast, mix and grind themselves, but a shop-bought mixture is fine.

Gram, or chickpea, flour A type of flour made from chickpeas. Available in large supermarkets, Indian and Middle Eastern shops.

Hoisin sauce A thick, brown, sweet and savoury sauce available from supermarkets and Chinese shops.

Kaffir lime leaves Can be bought dried, in a jar, from supermarkets; use them up quickly before they lose their magical fragrance.

Ketjap manis A type of soy sauce from Indonesia, which is sweeter and less salty than most other types. It can be found in large supermarkets. Alternatively, you can sweeten ordinary soy sauce with some honey. Store indefinitely in a cool, dry place.

Kombu Dried seaweed used for the preparation of Japanese stock. Available in Asian stores and health-food shops.

Kuzu (Japanese starch) Available in Japanese and health-food shops. Arrowroot or cornflour can be used instead.

Lemon grass Long, tapering grass-like stalks with a lemon flavour. Crush and cook in the recipe, then remove before serving, or remove the tough outer skin and use just the tender centre part, sliced.

Masa harina A type of cornmeal used to make tortillas. You can buy it at stockists of Mexican food and some large supermarkets.

Mirin A sweet fortified yellow Japanese wine used only for cooking. Found in Asian stores and some large supermarkets.

Miso Fermented soya paste. Generally speaking, the lighter the miso the milder the flavour and greater the sweetness. Available in healthfood shops and Asian stores. To get the full health benefits, buy unpasteurized miso and do not boil or overheat it in order to retain its health-giving enzymes.

Nori Seaweed, sold in flat sheets, for use in sushi rolls. Buy pretoasted nori from Asian and healthfood shops.

Nutritional yeast Dried 'inactive' yeast in the form of flakes, available in a tub from upmarket healthfood shops. It has a pleasant cheesy, nutty taste – and is rich in many nutrients.

Palm sugar A brown unrefined sugar used throughout Asia. It is available from large supermarkets and is often sold as a solid block. Soft dark brown muscovado sugar can be substituted.

Pastry From a health and flavour point of view, I prefer pure butter pastry. You can buy it from Dorset Pastry Company, www.dorsetpastry.com, who supply some upmarket shops. They make a puff pastry and a shortcrust pastry with cumin seeds, as well as other types.

Porcini mushrooms in white truffle oil Both truffle oil and porcini and white truffle paste can be found in large supermarkets or Italian food shops.

Ras el hanout A Moroccan spice mixture that you can buy at large supermarkets.

Rice vinegar A light, delicate vinegar made from rice wine. Available in large supermarkets and Asian shops. Wine vinegar (red or white) can be substituted, but use a little less.

Sake A pale golden wine made from rice, with 15–17% alcohol. Available in Asian shops. White wine or dry sherry can be substituted.

Sesame oil Dark sesame oil can be found in any supermarket and it gives a unique and delectable flavour to Asian dishes. You need only a small amount.

Shiitake mushrooms Chinese mushrooms, available fresh from many supermarkets and Asian shops.

Soya flour A type of flour made from soya beans. Available in supermarkets and healthfood shops.

Tahini Like peanut butter, but made from sesame seeds, without additives. I prefer the pale version, which is easy to find in supermarkets and healthfood shops.

Tamari, shoyu and soy sauce Shoyu is the Japanese word for soy sauce. It is an all-purpose flavouring enhancer; tamari is wheat-free with a stronger flavour. It's important to make sure you buy brands that are traditionally brewed, natural and organic. Available from some big supermarkets and from healthfood shops.

Tamarind A long brown pod with seeds and a tangy pulp used throughout Asia as a souring ingredient. Tamarind paste can be found in jars in Indian food shops and large supermarkets. Lemon juice can be used instead.

Tempeh A naturally fermented soya product, like tofu, but made from whole soya beans, rather than soya milk. Pale-coloured tempeh is usually the best to start with as it has the mildest flavour. Available in healthfood shops.

Teriyaki sauce A sweet sauce made from equal parts of soy sauce and mirin (or soy sauce, sake and sugar to taste). It is available in supermarkets and Asian shops, or you can mix your own.

Thai curry paste Most contain shrimp or other fish paste but vegetarian red and green curry paste is available in some supermarkets.

Tofu Tofu is found in the chilled food section of most supermarkets. The type most widely available is 'firm'. I've mostly used this in the recipes because it's a reliable all-purpose type of tofu, suitable for slicing and frying or, with liquid added, for making into a dip or dressing. You can buy other fine, delicate types of tofu in Asian food and organic shops and these are delicious and worth experimenting with if you like tofu.

Toover dhal Also called toor dhal, this is a small golden pulse. It has an earthy, almost smoky flavour and makes a beautiful dhal. Sometimes it's coated in oil to preserve it – wash this off by rinsing it in hot water before cooking. Yellow split peas would be the best substitute.

Umeboshi plums/umeboshi paste These have a delicious salty sharpness that enhances many foods. Refrigerated, they will last for ages in their jar. Buy from good healthfood shops.

Unsweetened soya cream Cartons of soya cream equivalent to single cream can be found in healthfood shops and supermarkets in the UK. It does contain a little sugar, but not enough to make it 'sweet' – check the label. In the USA it is not so easy to find substitute unsweetened soya milk, which has a creamy consistency when cooked. A ready-whipped soya cream in an aerosol, and another that you can whip yourself, have recently become available – I find them overly sweet.

Vege-Gel Vegetarian gelatine available from supermarkets. It's easy to use and sets very quickly.

Vegetable stock Marigold vegetable bouillon, a powder which comes in a tub, makes beautiful vegetable stock. Most supermarkets sell it, as do healthfood shops, and there is also a vegan version that doesn't contain lactose.

Vegetarian Worcestershire sauce Can be bought from healthfood shops. (The problem with ordinary Worcestershire sauce is that it contains anchovy extract.)

Vinegars While you can get away with just one type of vinegar – I'd choose organic cider vinegar – it's useful to have two or three different ones. Rice vinegar is light and suitable for Chinese and Japanese dishes, while balsamic has a wonderfully rich, sweet flavour: the more you spend on it, the better it will be.

Wakame seaweed A leafy seaweed, a bit like spinach to look at and with a mild, yummy flavour of the sea. Available dried from good healthfood shops.

Wasabi A strong green Japanese horseradish condiment with a hot mustard taste. It is available as a powder or a paste in large supermarkets and Asian shops. English mustard can be substituted.

Wild mushrooms Supermarket wild mushroom mixtures can be good value, though for a real treat and a no-expense-spared meal nothing can replace a few precious chanterelles, morels or some fresh porcini. Although they're very expensive, because they weigh very little you get a lot for your money. Dried mushrooms are good value – I especially like dried morels that you can buy at some big supermarkets.

Notes on the recipes

Frying

The healthiest way to deep-fry is to use rapeseed or groundnut oils, which are stable at high temperatures (and therefore healthier), and discard them after use. I use a wok, which has a large surface area so you use less oil or, if I'm doing just a little frying, a small saucepan. For shallow-frying and roasting I generally use olive oil, which is my standard all-purpose oil, but please refer to the individual recipe.

To grill and skin a red pepper

To grill and skin a red pepper, cut the pepper in half and remove the core, stem and seeds. Place the halves rounded-side up on a grill pan and grill on high for about 10 minutes, or until the skin is blistered and black in places and the flesh tender. Remove from the heat and leave to cool, then peel off the skin.

Toasting hazelnuts

If you're starting with the skinned type (which are the most widely available), either toast them under a hot grill for a few minutes, stirring them after 1–2 minutes so they toast evenly, or put them on a baking sheet and roast in a moderate oven – 180°C (350°F), Gas Mark 4. They'll take only 8–10 minutes, so watch them carefully and remove them from the hot baking sheet immediately they're done so they don't go on browning. To toast unskinned hazelnuts, that is, those still in their brown skins, proceed as described, but they'll take about 20 minutes in the oven. Let them cool, then rub off the brown skins with your fingers or a soft cloth.

Alcoholic drinks

Some wines and alcoholic drinks are prepared using animal by-products such as gelatine, although increasingly many are vegetarian or vegan. Read the label or check with the supplier to be sure.

Making recipes vegan

Many of the recipes in this book are naturally vegan and are labelled as such. A lot more can easily be made vegan by making simple substitutions such as using olive oil or vegan margarine instead of butter, soya instead of dairy cream, real maple syrup instead of honey, and vegan puff pastry (read the label) instead of all-butter puff pastry. Here are some suggested vegan alternatives:

Suggested vegan alternatives

NON-VEGAN	VEGAN
butter	vegan margarine
milk	soya milk
cream	soya cream
yogurt	soya yogurt
cream cheese	vegan cream cheese
goats' cheese	vegan cream cheese
feta cheese	vegan feta cheese
Cheddar (or other firm) cheese	vegan Cheddar (or other firm) cheese
Parmesan-style cheese (grated)	vegan Parmesan cheese
paneer	firm tofu or firm vegan cheese
mayonnaise	vegan mayonnaise
hollandaise sauce	vegan mayonnaise
honey	real maple syrup

Index

Author acknowledgements

Many talented people have been involved with the production of this book and I'd like to acknowledge them all. In particular, Eleanor Maxfield, commissioning editor, who had the initial idea and masterminded this book; Clare Churly, my editor, for her hard work; Jo Murray, who did such an excellent job on the proofs; Will Webb, for the beautiful new design; and also Jonathan Christie, Jennifer Veall and Katherine Hockley. It was so satisfying to see this book take shape from my two previous books – *Vegetarian Supercook* and *Veggie Chic* – and I'm thrilled with the result. I would also like to thank Sarah Ford, who commissioned those two books and worked closely with me, and the people who helped to produce them: Alison Goff, Sue Bobbermein, Tracy Killick, Jo MacGregor, Rachel Lawrence, Jessica Cowie, Barbara Dixon, Jo Lethaby, Ian Paton, Martin Crowshaw, Rachel Jukes, Liz Hippisley; and the wonderful photographers and food stylists, Gus Filgate and David Martin, who worked their genius for *Vegetarian Supercook*, and Jason Lowe and Sunil Vijayakar, who did the same for *Veggie Chic*. I'd also like to say a special 'thank you' to Ant Jones of Cliqq Photography and *Cook Vegetarian Magazine* for my photo; to my daughter Claire for her help with creating and testing recipes for *Veggie Chic*; to my agent Barbara Levy for all her help and advice; and to my dear husband Robert for mammoth washing up sessions and so much besides: Thank you all from my heart.

Picture acknowledgements

Octopus Publishing Group/Gus Filgate and Jason Lowe
Author portrait: Ant Jones/CliQQ Photography (www.cliqq.co.uk)

An Hachette UK Company
www.hachette.co.uk

First published in Great Britain in 2013 by
Hamlyn, a division of Octopus Publishing Group Ltd
Endeavour House
189 Shaftesbury Avenue
London
WC2H 8JY
www.octopusbooks.co.uk

ISBN 978-0-600-62584-1

A CIP catalogue record for this book is available from the British Library

Printed and bound in China

10 9 8 7 6 5 4 3 2 1

Commissioning Editor: Eleanor Maxfield
Managing Editor: Clare Churly
Art Director: Jonathan Christie
Design by Will Webb
Picture Library Manager: Jennifer Veall
Assistant Production Manager: Caroline Alberti